Welcome
to the Lord's Table

Text copyright © 1999, 2006 Margaret Withers
The author asserts the moral right
to be identified as the author of this work.

Published by
The Bible Reading Fellowship
First Floor, Elsfield Hall,
15–17 Elsfield Way, Oxford OX2 8FG

ISBN-10 1 84101 504 0
13-digit ISBN 978 1 84101 504 0

First edition 1999
This edition 2006
10 9 8 7 6 5 4 3 2 1 0
All rights reserved

Acknowledgments
Scripture quotations are taken from the Contemporary English Version Bible published
by HarperCollins Publishers, copyright © 1991, 1992, 1995 American Bible Society.

Material from *Common Worship* published by Church House Publishing, copyright ©
Archbishops' Council 2000

A catalogue record for this book is available from the British Library.

Printed in Singapore by Craft Print International Ltd

Welcome

to the Lord's Table

A practical course for preparing children
to receive Holy Communion

Margaret Withers

Acknowledgments

Thanks are due to:

the Revd Chris Dench, Assistant Director of Ministry and Training, CME and Vocation, for the diocese of Rochester; the staff and children of St Peter and St Paul, Leybourne, and its Church of England Primary School, who piloted some of the units;

the Revd Canon David Knight, Vicar of Ranmoor, Sheffield, and formerly Canon Precentor of Chelmsford Cathedral, who helped with liturgical matters in the original edition.

Contents

Foreword

To have the opportunity of talking to children is a huge privilege. To have the opportunity of talking with children is pure gift. Whenever we begin a conversation with a child, we are entering into an adventure, in which the adult is never quite sure where the talking is going to lead. The one thing that is sure is that we shall receive, grow and be amazed at least as much as the children.

The same is true when we talk with children about Jesus, for their relationship with him can have a freshness, an openness, an unexpectedness, a wonder, that rejuvenates our own longer-standing and more mature friendship with the Lord.

It is good that parishes up and down the country are beginning to discover what our Orthodox brothers and sisters have known for so long—that encouraging children and adults to receive Holy Communion together is pure gift from God to all of us. You only have to look at the face of a youngster at the altar rail to find your own awe and wonder at the sacrament immeasurably enriched. You only have to look at the face of a youngster at the altar rail to see what it means to them to be in the presence of the living Lord, kneeling alongside adults who recognize them as fellow members of the Body of Christ.

But this does not just happen. It is important that congregations are prepared for this adventure as much as the children.

I am particularly grateful to Margaret Withers for all the work she has done and is doing, along with her colleagues up and down the country, to encourage us to take our ministry and evangelism among children seriously. And I especially want to thank her for this revised version of *Welcome to the Lord's Table*, which provides us with such a rich treasure of ideas as adults and children together explore the scriptures and the breaking of the bread, and what it really means to say, 'We are the Body of Christ.'

I pray that we all might say with those disciples on the road to Emmaus, 'Then our eyes were opened, and we recognized him' in the scriptures, in the breaking of the bread, and in each other.

The Rt Revd Stephen Venner, Bishop in Cantervury and Bishop of Dover

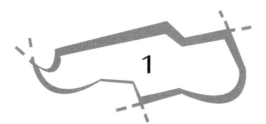

The Lord's command

A VISITOR TO SUPPER

'It started on the way home on Sunday,' he said. 'You know what it's like after a holiday. The road was packed with men, some with their wives and children, even a few animals. Everyone was anxious to get out of the city before the sun started going down or we would not get home before it was dark.

'It's hard to tell what we felt like: sort of numb with shock at what had happened. We had been sure that there was going to be some kind of revolution, and it had started well with this grand procession into town and everyone shouting and cheering. It was as if even the stones on the path were cheering with us! Then it all went wrong and, next thing we knew, he had been clapped into prison. We saw him the next morning, covered with blood and hardly recognizable, dragging his cross through the street. It just seemed unreal, like an awful dream; and then it was all over. He was dead.

'I don't think that we said much to each other on that journey. Every so often we would remember something Jesus had said or something he had done. Everything we had hoped for had fallen to bits and all we wanted to do was to get as far away from Jerusalem as possible and back to our families.

'Then this chap joined us. Neither of us really bothered to look at him. The setting sun was in our eyes and we were not in the mood for being friendly. He seemed a kindly sort of person and he asked us what was wrong. We tried to explain what had happened, but, before we got very far, he interrupted us. Said we'd got it all wrong and started to make us see it in another way. He must have been a rabbi or some kind of scholar because he knew the scriptures inside out, and he explained how everything we told him about Jesus could be linked with Moses and the prophets. We started getting really excited.

'Anyway, when we got to the village it was nearly dark, so we asked him to stay the night with us. And that's when it happened. We sat down to supper and this chap took the bread, said the blessing and handed it to us. And suddenly we looked at him properly. It was Jesus.'

Cleopas paused for a moment. 'Do you know,' he continued, 'all of our depression and fear just vanished. He was there, just as he always had been. And, somehow, I know that it will always be like that. Whenever we break bread and remember what he did for us, he will be there.'

KNOWN TO THEM IN THE BREAKING OF BREAD

Since that famous journey on the road to Emmaus, when two bereaved friends invited a stranger to share their family meal and recognized the risen Lord, groups of Jesus' followers have met him in the breaking of bread, in churches, chapels, the open air, schools and homes. Every minute, somewhere in the world, Christ's sacrifice on the cross is recalled. Whether it is as a glorious ceremony in a medieval cathedral or a scrap of black bread saved from meagre rations on a packing case in a prison hut, it is the definitive way in which the vast majority of Christians obey the Lord's command, 'Do this in remembrance of me.'

Closely aligned to this commandment is another: 'Love each other, as I have loved you' (John 15:12) and Jesus' own prayer that he wanted his disciples all 'to be one with each other… [so that] the people of this world will believe that you sent me' (John 17:21). It is tragic, therefore, that over the centuries the response to 'do this in remembrance of me' has been a source of division and hatred, leading to fragmented families and communities, even imprisonment and death.

SIGNS OF HOPE

But there are signs of hope. Christians are praying, studying and working together in a way that would not have been dreamed of 20 years ago. In rural areas, many Anglican churches are ecumenical in that they are the only place of worship for a community from varied religious traditions and backgrounds. In some urban areas, local ecumenical partnerships have flourished, with members of the congregation maintaining their distinctive traditions but 'hanging them up' at the door of the church building in order to work and pray together to the enrichment of all concerned.

At the same time, there has been a significant change in the pattern of Sunday worship in the whole Western church. In the Roman Catholic Church, the Mass, always the central service, became more accessible following the reforms of the Second Vatican Council. In the Church of England, the Eucharist is now established in the majority of parishes as the main Sunday service while, in the Free Churches, there are more frequent services of Holy Communion as a central act of worship with children present. All this has led to a rediscovery of eucharistic worship as the gathering together of the Lord's people on the Lord's day to celebrate his resurrection and meet him through the breaking of bread. Children who, 30 years ago, would have had little if any experience of this worship are now present Sunday by Sunday to hear the invitation, 'Draw near with faith… all those who love the Lord.' '… Happy are those who are called to his supper.' History, however, has decreed that, in the Anglican and Free Church traditions, children have been refused a full share in his banquet.

This is changing. Children are being admitted to Holy Communion for a variety of reasons. There has been a renewed emphasis upon baptism as the sacrament of initiation of our children as fellow members of the Body of Christ, not tomorrow's Christians to be tucked away in a hall until they know what 'it' is all about! The sacraments are being seen afresh as signs of God's grace being poured out to us to which we respond, not rites in which we principally act in our own strength.

Greater sharing of worship between traditions and cultures led to a demand for new church legislation to provide guidelines and consistency. In the Church of England, the order of baptism, confirmation and Holy Communion remains the norm, but, in 1997, the General Synod made provision for children to be admitted to Holy Communion before confirmation. This requires the permission of the bishop, who needs to be satisfied that the parish priest and the Parochial Church Council support the move, and that, where appropriate, ecumenical partners have been consulted. It is now Methodist Church policy to admit children to Holy Communion, and similar practice is taking place in some other denominations.

Admission to Holy Communion should always be seen in the context of a stage on the Christian journey, so children's leaders must make their church council aware of the full programme of initiation and nurture provided for the children, and gain its support. Further information on this is given in chapter 2, 'Preparing the congregation'.

A LONG WAY TO GO

There are, however, many questions about this historic move, some of which are discussed in chapter 2. There is also the inevitable untidiness and inconsistency of a church that is beginning to 'grow up' and make its own decisions according to what is right for its community while remaining within the structure and practice of the wider church.

Many adults, used to the pattern of teenage confirmation or membership, have emphasized the importance of cognitive understanding, and want guarantees that children who are admitted to Holy Communion will always receive worthily and remain faithful for the rest of their lives. While we should take reception of the sacraments seriously, if we erect barriers which are largely irrelevant as a way to restrict or control them, we may starve some of our most vulnerable Christians of this channel of God's grace and thereby impoverish the whole church and the society it aims to serve.

A FREE GIFT

God's grace is freely poured out and it is not for us to look at motives or calculate end results. Jesus healed ten lepers but only one returned to thank him (Luke 17:12–19). If he had to accept a ten per cent response rate to his gift, who are we to demand more?

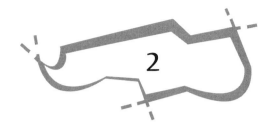

Preparing the congregation

Children being prepared to receive Holy Communion need the support and help of three groups of people: their families, their teachers or leaders, and the local church community. This community is usually the congregation gathered at church on Sunday, but may also be a Church school, or occasionally a midweek club which includes worship. If the practice is new, it will affect every person and many of the things that are done, starting with a major change of thought about children as part of the worshipping community. Views will be expressed which range from proscriptive statements about 'suitability' to sentimental comments about 'little hands being stretched out', neither of which is helpful. There will be worry about the disappearance of familiar structures but, also, excitement and a desire to know more.

open meeting so that everyone can feel informed and part of the process, are vital.

Subjects for teaching and discussion:

* What is baptism?
* Grace, not worthiness
* Discipleship
* Being part of the Church family
* 'Family Communion' or 'Adults Only'?
* Supporting Christian children—a vulnerable minority in their schools and social lives

A brief historical background, looking at the intentions of the Reformers and the developments in the Church during the last 30 years, may also be useful.

THIS INVOLVES THE WHOLE COMMUNITY

Christian nurture is not an individual matter, nor is it the rote learning of statements. It is the handing down of the faith of the Church to its children by sharing of experience and example as much as direct teaching: 'These are things we learnt from our ancestors, and we will tell them to the next generation. We won't keep secret the glorious deeds and the mighty miracles of the Lord' (Psalm 78:3–4).

Every member of the worshipping community is involved in this nurture at every occasion. The way the child sees each adult's faith expressed in worship of God and behaviour to other people will have far more lasting influence than all the preparation classes in the world.

If this is a new project, or even being considered, teaching through sermons, study groups, and maybe an

COMMON QUESTIONS WITH A FEW OF THE MANY ANSWERS

Why change at all?

The pattern produced by the Reformers, which has been inherited in some form by all the Reformed churches, dates from a time when everyone belonged to the Church and practice of religion was public. Church played a central part in the life of the whole community and this experience of belonging was the basis upon which the faith was taught. This is no longer the case. Practice of a religion is now largely an individual matter.

During the last 30 years, Holy Communion has become the central Sunday service in most Anglican and many Free churches where, hitherto, it had usually taken place either early in the morning or after the main worship. This has allowed children to join in celebrating the service that the Lord gave us. Then to exclude believing and baptized children from receiving Holy Communion negates the Church's teaching about baptism welcoming children into the Lord's family, and all that is done to give children a sense of belonging to the worshipping community.

Youngsters are maturing physically at a younger age, so they are coping with the problems of puberty and adolescence from about ten onwards. At the same time, they have the strains and time commitment of starting secondary school, with new subjects and teachers, homework and maybe a long journey.

Church attendance is now something for a small minority. Early teens are the worst age for any youngster to make a commitment which most of his or her peers will see as eccentric, when he or she is under pressure from extra-curricular activities and invitations to Sunday sporting events, outings and sleepovers.

Youngsters need the security of being full and welcome members of a Christian community, with the grace of the sacraments to support them through these tough years, or they may vote with their feet for the easier charms that are on offer.

Discuss

I hope that most of them will stay faithful. I know that there are one or two for whom this does not mean much, but it may be that one day, when one of them is asked to help to plan a robbery or something, he will say, 'I was brought up a Catholic and I know this is wrong' and walk away. Remembering that makes the struggle with the difficult ones worthwhile.

FIRST COMMUNION TEACHER AT AN RC PRIMARY SCHOOL IN SOUTH LONDON

How will children be selected and who decides whether they are suitable?

The request to be prepared for admission to Holy Communion should come from the child and his or her parents. Parental support and involvement are vital. This and the role of godparents and sponsors are discussed in chapter 4.

Having started on the programme, it should not be taken for granted that a child will complete it and be admitted to Holy Communion. Good attendance, interest and completion of tasks are fundamental. There may be reasons for a family to decide to withdraw the child or postpone completion of the course. Clergy and leaders should be aware of family situations and offer support when it is needed.

Age, or being part of a particular group or class, are the simplest forms of selection and ones that children can understand. From the age of about seven, children can learn what it means to be a Christian, a disciple of Jesus Christ. Many youngsters of that age have a vivid faith and trust in a loving God. On a practical note, most of them can read and write well enough to do the simple tasks at home with the help of their parents. However, it is important to treat any guideline based on age with flexibility, for pastoral reasons.

We should not put burdens upon children by demanding stricter criteria from them than we expect from adults.

This programme is about grace: God's generosity to us and our response to him. Children who are perceived as 'difficult' may be those who are most in need of this expression of God's love, which can change their lives. It cannot be earned and is not a prize for being good.

Discuss

'There must be some sort of rope for them to jump over'; 'How do we judge that they are ready?'; 'They may not behave well enough.' Are the same criteria voiced about adults, or is the community welcoming to adult enquirers and genuinely moved by the coming to faith of the most reprobate sinner?

'The children sometimes giggle when they are blessed; should we allow them to receive Holy Communion if they behave like that?' Is this a concern about the children's attitude, or is it looking for a way to address the problem of the adults who whisper throughout the whole administration?

Will they understand what they are doing?

This is part of a programme that continues past first Holy Communion until confirmation and beyond. Leaders and parents should help their children to grow in their understanding of the significance of Holy Communion as part of their teaching and nurture.

It is discernment of the sacrament that is important. People who are unable to articulate their understanding should still be given the opportunity to experience the sacramental signs of God's love.

Discuss

In a psychiatric hospital, patients with mental ages of between three and nine years were prepared for the sacraments. The bishop had visited them before the service and spent time with each one of the candidates so that they got to know him. The devotion

on the part of those who were taking part was moving and the service was a real celebration that they all enjoyed. 'It is discernment of the sacrament that matters, not articulation of understanding.'

REPORT FROM A HOSPITAL CHAPLAIN

This does not involve us, so why are we discussing it?

Christians from cultures or denominations where the children are admitted to Holy Communion are playing a full part within our congregations. Many of them have children who are communicants.

We live in a society where much of the population is transient. Families move around the country for career or social reasons in a way that was unheard of 30 years ago. Children who have been admitted to Holy Communion in their home parish may move into your area and arrive in your church. According to the Church of England's review in 2005, *Children and Holy Communion*, about eleven per cent of parishes admit children to Holy Communion and the number is increasing steadily. A family with communicant children may come to your church at any time. It is important that the congregation recognizes the children's communicant status and is aware of the background.

The Christian community should emphasize the importance of Holy Communion, through example, by valuing its ministry with children and providing good-quality resources for their nurture. This involves interest, funding and regular discussion by the church council.

Discuss

An Anglican family was worshipping within a Local Ecumenical Project where the children were welcomed at Holy Communion as baptized and nurtured Christians. They moved to a village where they wanted to become part of the life of the parish church but experienced the pain of their children being excluded from the sacrament and the children's own bewilderment at their perceived rejection by a church of which they thought they were members.

A PARENT IN NORTH ESSEX

A new priest arrives from South Africa. His two children are too young to be confirmed but have been admitted to Holy Communion, so receive it every Sunday. Children being admitted to Holy Communion had not been discussed in this church.

CHURCH IN AN INNER CITY

How would you react if either of these families came to your church?

What will happen to confirmation?

It is hoped that confirmation will come to be seen as a sacrament in its own right rather than a procedure to be gone through in order to receive Holy Communion. Some bishops place commitment to eventual confirmation at the heart of their permission for children to be admitted as communicants. A pattern of communicant children being confirmed during their late teens is beginning to emerge. This is being seen as an adult affirmation of faith as well as the reception of the grace of the Holy Spirit.

The laying on of hands and reception of the Holy Spirit were often linked with commissioning or 'sending out' (apostleship) in the early Church, so this would be appropriate for youngsters who are beginning to take responsibility in the Christian community, starting their first jobs or going to university.

While they were worshipping the Lord and going without eating, the Holy Spirit told them, 'Appoint Barnabas and Saul to do the work for which I have chosen them.' Everyone prayed and went without eating for a while longer. Next, they placed their hands on Barnabas and Saul to show that they had been appointed to do this work. Then everyone sent them on their way. (Acts 13:2–3)

THINK AND DISCUSS

- ❖ Does our community provide a welcoming and secure environment for the children to grow in faith?
- ❖ Is the whole congregation aware of its corporate responsibility for the nurture of the children by prayer and example as well as teaching?
- ❖ Are we providing continuous support and nurture for our young people?
- ❖ If the answer to any of the above is 'No', what is the best way to start bringing about change?
- ❖ Is there a need for special teaching or a meeting to address questions and fears from the congregation?

3

Training the leaders

WHO WILL TEACH THE CHILDREN?

It is often assumed that preparation for the sacraments is the job of the priest or minister. He or she has the responsibility for the teaching and nurture of all of the congregation and it has been argued that, as the professional, she or he alone has the knowledge and authority to carry out this most important teaching. If, however, she or he takes the teaching aspect of ministry seriously and encourages all forms of study and training, it should, in turn, produce lay leaders who have a clear understanding of the Christian faith and can exercise a teaching ministry in all sorts of activities: study groups, youth and children's work, baptism, Holy Communion and marriage preparation.

The role of the clergy

In some churches, the priest or minister may be a skilled and inspiring teacher. He or she may have been a teacher at some time or have other experience in the training field. If this is the case, there is every reason for the minister to use these talents and to form a relationship with each child and family at an important stage in their lives.

Clergy, however, have many commitments and conflicting demands. If they are teaching children, they should always have at least one other person working alongside them (one of whom should be female) to provide support and to ensure that basic health and safety procedures are carried out. Maintaining a ratio of at least two adults to every eight children will mean that help is always to hand if a child becomes ill or distressed. It will also ensure that sessions are not cancelled because of emergencies or personal illness.

Whoever is teaching the course, the clergy should discuss the programme with them, attend planning meetings and provide general support. They should also make opportunities to get to know the children and their families by attending some sessions, and visiting their homes if appropriate.

In school

If the preparation is taking place in a school, the best person to lead the group may be the teacher who is responsible for worship or RE. He or she could work alongside the clergy. Teachers will meet the children on a daily basis and know them well. If parents do not regularly attend worship at church or the school, it could be appropriate for a member of staff to act as a sponsor. This is a major commitment and is discussed in chapter 4.

Using lay leaders

In all denominations, the tradition is for the laity to have responsibility for the children's work, and there is every reason for preparation for Holy Communion to follow the same pattern with the support and overview of the priest or minister:

- In a church, the children's teaching usually takes place during the Sunday morning when the clergy are leading the main worship. Some of the preparation for Holy Communion may also take place at this time. Extra teaching, maybe after school, will be more effective if the leaders and children are already known to each other. This might take place at the local school if all the children are students there.
- Using lay leaders or school teachers affirms the value of the work done by the leaders who nurture the children week by week, and the witness of Christian teachers, as well as encouraging high standards for all of the children's work.
- It is a way of showing that the children's nurture is an ongoing process which involves the whole Christian family.
- The priest or minister may not relate well to young children or understand the sort of teaching that they need, but there may be several people in the congregation with teaching or communication skills who would be ideal as leaders.

Although this course provides the organization and structure for a group of about ten children, it is recognized that in many cases the group will be smaller. It is important to keep the same standards of care, however small the group. As already stated, for health and safety reasons, a group should have at least two leaders, one of whom should be female.

What sort of people do we need?

Many churches select their teachers and leaders with great care. Others are grateful for anyone who volunteers. A checklist based on that used by local authorities is a useful guideline.

Recommended criteria for all people who work with children

The following criteria are based on the Home Office guidelines, *Safe from Harm*. For more information, visit the website www.homeoffice.gov.uk/docs/harm.html.

1. Previous experience of looking after or working with children or young people. If there is no such experience, the leader should be willing to undertake training within the first twelve months.
2. The ability to provide warm and consistent care.
3. A willingness to respect the background and culture of all children in their care.
4. A commitment to treat all children and young people as individuals and with equal concern.
5. Reasonable physical health, mental stability, integrity and flexibility.

In addition to this, all new leaders should be approved by the church council and have undergone the Criminal Records Bureau (CRB) enhanced disclosure. This is usually processed by your diocesan or denominational office, who will provide any advice that the church council needs.

FINDING AND ENABLING LEADERS AND HELPERS

It is usually better to seek out and invite people to help with children's work than to wait for volunteers. There may be somebody longing to be asked, or other people who do not realize they have all the skills required, so do not put themselves forward.

Caring for children is a big responsibility and some people are reluctant to volunteer in case they cannot cope with a band of lively youngsters. Someone who is starting to work with children should work alongside an experienced leader for guidance and be offered training according to his or her needs.

It is vital for a prospective leader or helper to meet with the clergy and other leaders to discuss the work and commitment, so that everyone knows what is expected.

The church council should be informed about all changes of leaders and new helpers. Remembering them in the prayers or a simple rite of commissioning at the main service reminds the congregation of the importance of this work and the need for positive and prayerful support.

Before seeking out leaders, or assuming that you will use the present ones, think through what is required and what are the aims of the work. A useful exercise is to draw up a mock advertisement (see overleaf) and job description as a way of identifying the sort of people you need and the work involved. The role of the church council as the body with responsibility for all that goes on in the church should also be identified.

How do the leaders get resources and training?

Training can take many forms:

- Regular meetings to plan and monitor the work, as well as discussing needs and problems, are the minimum requirement. *Welcome to the Lord's Table* is designed to be flexible and so can be used in a variety of ways. It is vital that, the first time it is used, leaders meet frequently to discuss which parts to use and to monitor timing and the children's response.
- Meetings could include a short session on a particular skill or subject by one of the group, a member of the congregation or an outside expert. If this is done over a meal, it adds a social dimension and helps to acknowledge the value of the work being done.
- Training and resources are provided by diocesan and denominational staff as well as organizations like BRF or Scripture Union. Each diocese or district should have a designated person whose job it is to provide training to suit the needs of a particular situation.
- Regular reading of the scriptures, membership of a study group or the guidance of a spiritual director ensure that the leader's own faith stays alive and is constantly challenged.

An annual quiet day or session away from the church to reflect upon the ministry of working with children is of great value.

WANTED:
LEADERS

for *Welcome to the Lord's Table*, our children's Communion course

Christ Church, Newtown, is seeking Christian adults, preferably established members of the congregation, to lead a group of children aged 7–9 years in their exploration of their faith before receiving Holy Communion. This is an integral part of our children's Christian formation and will take place during the Sunday morning service and during the Disciples' Club, which is held on Wednesdays after school.

Children are valued members of this church and their care and nurture are among our most important ministries. We expect our leaders to be people to whom we can entrust our children, knowing that they will ensure the safety and well-being of each of the youngsters in their care. Applicants should be able to share their own faith through their teaching, to speak with confidence about God's saving grace and the good news of Jesus Christ, and to be positive role models.

Formal qualifications are not required, but leaders will be expected to give time to preparation and attend a monthly planning meeting, led by one of the clergy. If prospective applicants have not had any training or experience of working with children, the church will pay for them to attend a short basic course and have further training as required. The whole team will spend an awayday at the Emmaus Centre each June. The work is time-consuming and often goes unnoticed but the church council will support it with its prayers and financial help. The main reward, however, will be helping the children to grow in faith as part of God's family and come to know and love the Lord Jesus though meeting him in Holy Communion Sunday by Sunday.

Apply to:
The Rev'd John Kirk
01586 717360

NB: The post is subject to a Criminal Records Bureau enhanced disclosure.

THINK AND DISCUSS

- ❖ Do we have the best people available doing our children's work at present?
- ❖ Do we do everything we can to see that our children are cared for and valued?
- ❖ Can we identify suitable people who could be invited to join the team?
- ❖ What sort of support and training should we make available to enable the leaders to use and develop their skills?
- ❖ Is the church council owning this work by providing realistic support and funding?

4

Involving the family

THE PARENTAL ROLE

Preparation to receive Holy Communion is not just something for a group of children to do on Sunday morning, or a special course lasting a few weeks. It is part of the passing on of the Christian faith, both the traditions that have been handed down and our personal experiences of Holy Communion, to the next generation of Christians. Our faith will make most sense to the children when it is acted out in the context of the family. It is in that relationship that the children should experience a glimpse of God's unconditional love for us through our serving each other in daily life, when we are unwell, sad and lonely, as well as in celebrations. *Welcome to the Lord's Table* is a programme in which parents are involved at every stage in preparing their children for admission to Holy Communion.

In order for parents to support their children, it is important that they know what commitment is involved and that they understand what sort of things the children are learning. Four things are vital for this process:

- An introductory meeting for parents and other interested parties.
- Teaching for parents who want to learn more about their faith in order to help their children.
- Regular information on the progress of the course and special events.
- Personal contact with each family so that any fears or concerns can be addressed.

A wonderful evangelistic opportunity

For some parents, who only attend church occasionally, their child's asking to be admitted to Holy Communion may be the start of a renewal of their own faith. Such parents, and many others, may feel insecure about their own beliefs so it would be a good idea to run a short course on the basics of Christian faith and practice at the same time. This could be by parents joining a confirmation group, having a special course like Alpha or Emmaus, or simply by holding a discussion group based on the elements of *Welcome to the Lord's Table*.

USING SPONSORS

In the Church of England, the regulations state that parents have to give permission for their child to be admitted to Holy Communion. There are, however, many reasons why parents who want a Christian upbringing for their children, and are happy to support them, do not attend church regularly. Personal illness, having to work on Sundays or night shifts are the most obvious reasons, and these are exacerbated in a single-parent family or when only one parent is a committed Christian. Children who go to church with other relatives, neighbours or school friends may show equal commitment to those whose family worships together as a matter of course.

There are several situations in which it would be pastorally sensitive to suggest appointing a sponsor to provide support or extra help. The ideal person would be a godparent but, sadly, many godparents do not have the commitment themselves and/or do not live locally. Another relative, a family friend, the parent of a child who has done the course, or one of the congregation known to the child would be good choices. Whoever is invited to take on this role must be clear that their support is not needed just through the few weeks of the course but will be ongoing—in fact, a similar role to that of a godparent.

Identifying sponsors

The role of sponsor is a sensitive one involving close contact between an adult and a young child. The child must agree wholeheartedly to the choice of sponsor, as he or she is the one who will be the centre of the relationship. The parents must be fully involved in the process and on no account should a person who is not well known to the family be used. Our children are precious and are also among the most vulnerable members of our church community, so their needs and welfare must always be the first priority. If clergy need guidance on the choice of sponsors or people to provide practical help, it would be advisable to use the guidelines for the appointment of children's leaders in chapter 3.

PLANNING AN INFORMATION MEETING

- Give plenty of notice of the meeting and arrange it at a time that most parents can manage.
- If you know that several parents will have come straight from work, have coffee and light snacks available as a practical welcome.
- Provide some supervised activities for brothers and sisters so that the parents can be on their own during the session.
- Prepare a list of the dates and events in the course so that parents can plan work schedules and holidays.
- Have copies of the course, *Welcome to the Lord's Table*, and the children's activity book, available. The course uses the Contemporary English Version Bible (CEV), so have a few copies of it to sell to parents who do not have a modern version of the Bible.
- Questions will be asked about how much time should be spent on tasks at home, how much help should be given, and what standard is required, so have your answers ready.

A suitable invitation to the meeting would look something like this:

CHRIST CHURCH, NEWTOWN

The parents of

....

are invited to attend an information meeting about preparation for Holy Communion at:

Christ Church Hall, Market Street, Newtown

Tuesday 10 January at 7.30pm

Light refreshments will be served from 7 o'clock

Crèche facilities will be provided by the 2nd Newtown Guides under the leadership of:
Diana Green, tel: 01586 672593, and Jo Lester, tel: 01586 678211

The parents of all children aged seven or over next birthday who are connected with Christ Church are welcome, so please make this invitation known to your friends.

For further details, contact Rev'd John Kirk on 01586 717360

At the meeting

Introduce the group leaders to the parents and explain how the course operates and how the parents are involved. Points to mention are:

- The child should have been baptized and the parents must give written permission for him or her to start the course.
- If a child has not been baptized but wishes to receive Holy Communion, he or she could be prepared for baptism at the same time. It is important to ensure that children who have not been baptized as babies are given this opportunity.
- Commitment is required from the parents in seeing that the children attend sessions, helping with the tasks to be done at home and attending church with them. The clergy and leaders need to be aware of situations that make this difficult, such as a child from a split family visiting the other parent, and ensure that the child is not excluded for reasons beyond his or her control.
- If parents feel that they cannot make this commitment on their own, they may speak to the leader privately to see if it would be appropriate to provide a sponsor, discussion group or other assistance.
- The activity book is there to help the children to learn, and all we (and God!) require from them is that they do their best. The children should be encouraged to take a pride in the activity books because they may be presented at the admission to Holy Communion service as a symbol of the children offering themselves to God.
- As the children are part of the church family, the church should pay for the resources needed for the course.

Once the course has started, there are always opportunities to review the situation if the parents or leaders feel that a child is not sufficiently interested, or if a family situation makes it better to postpone admission to Holy Communion until the following year.

You may wish to provide a form for parents or guardians to confirm their own commitment, such as the sample below.

CHRIST CHURCH, NEWTOWN

We/I wish our/my child

....,

who has/has not been baptized, to join the group which is preparing to receive Holy Communion for the first time on Easter Sunday.

We/I undertake to see that he/she attends the course regularly and promise to take a full part in his/her preparation to receive Holy Communion.

We/I would like to discuss this commitment more fully with one of the clergy.
Yes/No

Signed _____

Parent(s)/Guardian(s)

Address _____

_____

An information sheet for parents would look something like this:

CHRIST CHURCH, NEWTOWN

Parents' notes on admission to Holy Communion course

The course for preparing children to receive Holy Communion will be starting on Sunday 22 January and will be held in the church hall in Market Street on Sunday mornings within the Junior Church and on Wednesdays from 4 to 5pm as part of the Disciples' Club. Children are expected to attend all of the sessions and to let the leader know in advance if they are ill or on holiday.

The leader will be Liz Viner, helped by Michelle Wheatcroft and Peter Stone. Our assistant priest, the Revd Alex Parson, will also be taking part.

The children will be using the course, *Welcome to the Lord's Table*. This is in ten units and includes occasions when the children will be especially involved in the Sunday service. Each child will have an activity book with a simple task to do at the end of each unit. This usually involves drawing or writing, but it may include finding out things about themselves, their families and the Christian faith. Please help them and talk about the work with them.

During the Disciples' Club meetings on Wednesdays, there will be a parents' discussion group in the back room so that you can find out more about the faith and ask questions related to the course. Everyone is welcome. There is also a Bible study group on Tuesday evenings, details of which are on the weekly notice sheet.

Please note the following dates:

22 January	Course starts (NB: There will be no Disciples' Club on 15 February as it is half term)
19 February	'Welcome and Presentation of Bibles' during the 10.30 service
19 March at 3.30pm	'Celebrating God's Forgiveness' followed by tea in the hall
5 April at 7.30pm	Rehearsal for first Holy Communion service. Parents and sponsors should attend this with their children
Easter Sunday	Admission to Holy Communion during the 10.30 Eucharist, followed by a celebration in the hall
26 April	Final session of the course

Children are welcome to continue as members of the Disciples' Club after they have completed the course. There will be a visit to the Superbowl at Oldville followed by a picnic lunch on 22 May. Details to follow.

Please contact me or one of the clergy if you have any queries or problems.

Signed: Elizabeth M. Viner

Liz Viner, 17a Park View, Newtown, 01586 674471

INVISIBLE SUPPORT

Many of our congregations are invisible—people who are housebound or in residential care, but who are faithful Christians, relying on home Communion, the occasional visitor and the church magazine to keep them attached to the worshipping community. A lively link with the church could be forged by asking such people to support a particular child as a prayer partner. As with choosing leaders, care must be taken to see that appropriate people are chosen to give support and that the child and his or her parents are happy with the contact. A brief description of the child, which could be a copy of the activity from Unit 1, 'Who am I?', and a photo may be well received if all parties, including the child, are happy for this to be given to the prayer partner.

KEEPING THE CHURCH FAMILY INFORMED

Having explained the commitment required from parents, the support that can be given by sponsors, and individual offers of prayer and other help, the wider church family needs the opportunity to be involved:

- Regular mention in prayers and on the notice sheet makes the course an integral part of the life of the church.
- Involving the candidates in the main worship is also a help. Sometimes the children will be focusing on a particular part of the service and this could be announced or incorporated in the sermon. A simple welcome ceremony and presentation of a Bible after Unit 4 has been completed should take place during the main service. See 'Marking the Journey', pages 41–43.
- Photographs and names could be displayed towards the end of the course (with parental consent) when it is certain which children will be admitted to Holy Communion. This could be a display, or you could use artwork based on one of the many biblical analogies to describe our membership of the Body of Christ, such as:
  - A vine branch with a picture on each leaf: 'I am the vine, and you are the branches' (John 15:5).
  - A church building with pictures in the brick outlines: 'You are living stones that are being used

to build a spiritual house' (1 Peter 2:5). Names of members of the congregation, local churches and mission links could be put on the other leaves or bricks, as well as names of saints to remind us that we are all part of the same Church on earth and in heaven.

- Instructions for making the above displays are given in Unit 10, on pages 75–76.

THINK OR DISCUSS

- ❖ Have we got our course planned in sufficient detail for parents to feel fully informed?
- ❖ Are we making clear what help is required from parents? Are we providing support where it is needed?
- ❖ Are we aware of any families on the fringe of our church for whom this may be an opportunity for them to become more involved or renew their faith? How do we respond to this?
- ❖ Who is going to organize publicity for the course to families, sponsors and the whole congregation?

Guide to the course

INTRODUCTION

Welcome to the Lord's Table is a course of ten units, with three services, 'Marking the Journey', and a final session, 'Looking to the Future', to record the children's progression through it. It is intended for children aged between 7 and 9 years but children of 10 years could also use it with additional discussion within the activities.

The course is designed to last about three months with the children receiving Holy Communion towards the end of it, but it could also be used as a junior confirmation course or in individual units for teaching a particular subject. It is not a complete course in the Christian faith. It is assumed that the children have a foundation knowledge that they have learned at home, through attending the Junior Church, or at school, and that nurture will continue after the course is completed.

Each unit is self-contained and designed for two sessions, each lasting about 40 minutes, with simple tasks to be done at home in an activity book (see 'Planning a timetable' on page 22 for details). It is possible to swap around the order of the sessions: for example, Unit 1, 'Who am I?' could be followed by Unit 3, 'God's family'. The course is designed for the children to receive Holy Communion after completing Unit 10 and to have the final unit soon after that. Unit 5, 'Jesus' friends', and Units 8 and 9, 'Jesus is risen' and 'Let's have a party', could be postponed until after the children have received Holy Communion.

Similarly, a unit may be taught to fit in with the season or Gospel of the day. It is assumed that the children will be present for part of the Eucharist on most Sundays. Some units feature sections of it, so the youngsters will reinforce what they have learned by being involved in the worship.

Note: The term 'Eucharist' or 'eucharistic worship' is used for any service that includes Holy Communion. 'Holy Communion' is used for the actual sacrament or the part of the service in which it is received.

THE UNITS

1. Who am I?
2. Jesus, our friend and brother
3. God's family
4. God's storybook
5. Jesus' friends
6. Thank you; please
7. Sorry!
8. Jesus is risen
9. Let's have a party
10. Let's share a meal

'Marking the Journey'

- Welcome and presentation of Bibles (following Unit 4)
- Celebrating God's forgiveness (following Unit 7 or 8)
- The first Holy Communion service (following Unit 10)
- Looking to the future: all that I am (at the end of the course)

Suggestions are given for the services, as well as guidance on planning and rehearsal.

Each unit comprises two teaching sessions, several activities, things that happen in church, worship, and a task in the activity book to be done at home. It also has paragraphs about preparation, resources needed and follow-up for the leaders.

Scripture

The course is centred on storytelling and relating the stories in scripture to the children's lives. Each session contains at least one portion of scripture, usually from Mark's Gospel, but readings from the other Gospels and the Psalms are also used. Quotations are taken from the Contemporary English Version of the Bible, or sometimes the author's paraphrase of it has been used. Alternatively, read from a child's book of Bible stories, or use your own words, especially with the youngest children.

Contents of each unit

Aim
Objectives
I believe (Apostles' Creed)
Biblical basis
Teaching time
Focus on church
Music
Prayer
Activities, which will include:

Drama
Game
Craft
Finding out

Tasks (to be done in the activity book)
Further action for leaders

Worship

As the course is designed to help the children to grow in faith and knowledge of God, worship through prayer and music is a vital component of every session. If the group meets on Sunday as well as a weekday, it is better to focus more on this during the weekday meeting as the Sunday session will probably include going into church to join in the corporate worship.

If the group is small and meets in a room, finish each session with a time of quiet, followed by the prayer and a hymn or song. If it meets in a larger space,

the children could sit in a circle with a focal point like a cross or a lighted candle. Quiet taped music can also have a calming effect after a lively session and help to set a reflective atmosphere. However the worship is done, time should be allowed for it to be done well, to sum up the session by offering it to God.

Prayer

There are suggestions for prayer in each unit. Some of them are responsorial as a way of helping the children to make them their own, but the units gradually move towards encouraging the children to adopt a natural and relaxed attitude towards prayer by praying aloud some of the things that they want to tell God about. This can be done at any session by asking the children what they want to thank God for or what concerns they have and, after a moment of quiet, collecting them up by saying the Lord's Prayer or singing a song.

Guard against directing or commenting about the children's prayers. God wants to hear what they say, not what you think they ought to say!

The Lord's Prayer

The Lord's Prayer features in several of the worship sessions and is printed in the activity book. It is accepted that different versions are used by different traditions. The version given in the activity book is widely used, but if it is not the one that your church uses, please adapt it by sticking your own version over it.

Music

Each unit includes suggestions for hymns or songs which can be used as an activity to reinforce the teaching or as part of the worship. It is not an exhaustive list, but gives a few suggestions from books that are commonly used in primary schools. There will also be traditional hymns that you may want to use. The abbreviations used refer to the following books:

CHE: *Celebration Hymnal for Everyone*, Patrick Geary (McCrimmons)
CP: *Come and Praise*, Geoffrey Marshall-Taylor (BBC)
JP: *Junior Praise*, Horrobin and Leavers (HarperCollins)
SSL: *Someone's Singing, Lord*, Beatrice Harrop (A&C Black)

Find out which hymns or songs the children know and let them lead the singing. If you decide to teach a new piece of music, sing or play the melody first, before adding chords or accompaniment, as children respond better to a single line of music. If the leader lacks the confidence to teach it on his or her own, ask someone to make a tape of a few hymns with the melody played line by line and, finally, the finished version.

PLANNING A TIMETABLE

The course is designed for each unit to consist of two sessions of about 40 minutes each. Care must be taken to allow adequate time for discussion and practical work.

The time needed has been indicated at the start of each section, but this is only a rough guide as much will depend on the age, abilities and size of the group. The talents of the leaders and resources available need to be taken into account when deciding which activities to do and how much emphasis to give to them. If the children have been part of the church family for several years and have learnt the basics of the Christian faith through worship as well as the Junior Church, much of the teaching in the first five units will probably be familiar. It may be best just to revise the subject with a brief question-and-answer session and consolidate it with an activity.

The timetable can be planned in several different ways according to the needs of the group. Children often have several commitments in the early evenings and the availability of leaders and venues has also to be considered. If some of the teaching takes place on Sunday morning, it is assumed that the session will last about 40 minutes and that the children will then go into the main service. Sunday afternoon, the time of the traditional Sunday school, or Saturday morning are both possibilities if it is not possible to find a time after school when the whole group is available.

There are three different ways of organizing a unit:

1. Two sessions each week:
   - Weekday after school: First session, activity and worship
   - Sunday morning: Second session, activity and 'Focus on church'

   or
   - Sunday morning: First session, activity, 'Focus on church'
   - Weekday after school: Second session, activity and worship

2. One weekly session covering the entire unit:
   - The session might take place on a weekday after school or in the early evening, or on a Saturday

morning or Sunday afternoon. If this pattern is followed, have a short break with some refreshments in the middle and allow about 90 minutes, finishing with 'Focus on church' and worship. This will probably be the best solution if the group is being run at school or includes children who cannot be present every Sunday for family reasons, or who sing in the choir or are servers.

3. Two Sunday morning sessions for each unit:
   - If this pattern is used, a unit will take a fortnight to complete. It has the disadvantage that the time is firmly fixed, so needs careful planning, and that the course will take about six months to complete.

If the children have a session immediately after school, or the course is run with a whole unit being studied in a single meeting, have someone available to prepare refreshments for both the children and the leaders.

Deciding which parts to do

Sections of each unit may be selected according to time and need but should always include:

- Both teaching sessions, adapted according to the knowledge of the group
- At least one activity
- 'Focus on church'
- Worship
- The task

Choose which activities to include according to the size and composition of the group as well as the local situation. Drama will be an appropriate choice in a church that uses it within its worship, if sessions have been planned to allow time for rehearsals, but a small group meeting in a room will gain more from the 'finding out' sessions or craft activities. Music can be used as an activity if time is short, to consolidate a 'finding out' session, or as part of the worship. Whatever is chosen, have as much variety as possible to cater for everyone's interests and skills.

Should opportunities arise that add to the quality of the course, such as being present at a baptism or using drama or music in a service, these should be grasped and the course adjusted by having an extra session at the end of the programme. We have already noted that some sessions can be postponed until after the children have received Holy Communion.

LANGUAGE

Welcome to the Lord's Table is designed to be used by Christians of all traditions, so it aims to use language that is broad enough to be acceptable to everyone. For clarity, the following terms are used:

- *Altar table* is ecumenically acceptable, so it is the only term used for the altar or Communion table.
- *Body of Christ* is used to describe the people of God, especially in the context of service.
- *Church*. When a capital 'C' is used, the word refers to the universal Church or a whole denomination, like the Methodist Church. When lower case is used, it refers to the local church, as a Christian community or a building.
- *Clergy* is used to mean the ordained person when possible. When not, 'priest or minister' will be used.
- *Congregation* is used to describe the people present in church every Sunday and is linked to leadership and decision-making.
- *Eucharist* or *eucharistic worship* is any service that includes Holy Communion.
- *Holy Communion* is used for the actual sacrament and the part of the service in which it is received.
- *Belonging* is used whenever possible to denote being part of the universal Church.
- *Parent* implies one or both of the natural or adoptive parents of the child, but, except for legal or official requirements such as parental permission needing to be given, it may include a guardian, sponsor or other relation who is supporting the child through the course.
- *Service* is more formal than 'act of worship': the main service is a Eucharist; the meeting started with an act of worship.
- *Worshipping community* is a slightly broader term than 'congregation' and is used largely in a pastoral context.

PREPARATION AND RESOURCES

If the course is to run smoothly, regular planning and evaluation are vital, especially with inexperienced leaders. It is probably best to meet to evaluate a group of about three units and to prepare the next block rather than to prepare the whole programme at once.

A vital part of planning and evaluation is a quick five minutes after each session, when comments and suggestions are easily called to mind.

However you organize your planning, keep some short notes about anything that goes wrong or especially well, for reporting later or noting before you do the course again.

This is a practical course, so see that someone has responsibility for assembling the resources and putting the displays in church. Many an activity has collapsed because something simple such as paper clips or water was forgotten, so this job is very important! It need not be done by a leader: some practical-minded person in the congregation may be happy to make it his or her contribution to the course.

Outline drawings of items are required for a few of the craft activities. It is not necessary to be an expert artist to produce them. Some may be copied from the activity book and others may be downloaded from the Internet. Every unit has a list of resources needed for the activities. Basic materials that will be needed almost every time are not listed. Make a 'Ready Box' so that you have them assembled for each session. Contents should include:

- A cross or candle as a focal point for worship
- A roll of wallpaper for the displays
- Drawing paper
- Pencils and sharpener
- Felt-tipped pens
- Scissors
- Adhesive sticks
- Drawing-pins or Blu-tack
- Newspaper to protect surfaces
- Rubbish bag

Arrange to have access to a tape or CD player, as you may want to include recorded music as part of the worship session. Make sure you know where equipment such as dustpans and brushes are kept.

The children will not usually need Bibles as the sessions are based on storytelling rather than reading, but you may like them to bring the ones that are presented to them and join in reading or following the story if the exact text is being used.

THE TASKS

The course is run in conjunction with the *Welcome to the Lord's Table* activity book. This is largely pictorial, with spaces for filling in words, short sentences and drawings. Each unit has a task that should be done at home. The advantage of this is that it allows children to work at their own pace and can also involve their parents. If a child needs extra help or the parents have difficulty in providing the support needed, it may be appropriate to use a sponsor from the congregation as suggested in Chapter 4.

The activity book is part of the child's offering to God, which they may present at their first Holy Communion service, so they should all be encouraged to take pride in their books. On the other hand, the work should never be marked competitively or used as a measure of a child's spiritual growth. Be aware of children who find writing difficult or have other special needs and see that instructions are always clear and to the point, or ask their parents for advice.

THINK AND DISCUSS

- ❖ Which will be the best way to operate the course? Are there any special situations we have to bear in mind? For example, a child who cannot be present every Sunday for family reasons or because of other commitments, or difficulty in getting children from a particular school to a midweek session?
- ❖ How will the course fit in with the present programme of nurture in our Junior Church or Sunday school?
- ❖ Which version of scripture or book of Bible stories shall we use? Shall we present the same version to the children when they receive their Bibles?
- ❖ Who will find out which hymns and songs the children use in school?
- ❖ How and when shall we meet to plan the work and evaluate past sessions?
- ❖ Who will order the activity books and Bibles?
- ❖ Who will take charge of providing resources for each session and organizing any displays?
- ❖ Who will see that the hall or room is booked and is set out before each session?

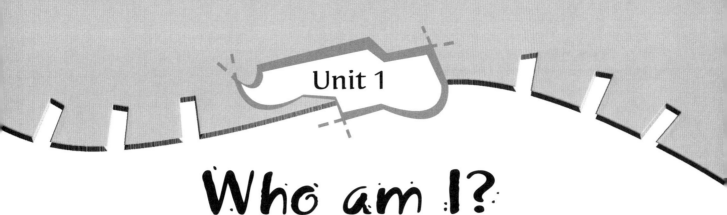

Unit 1

Who am I?

Aim

To recognize that each person is a unique individual on a journey through life.

Objectives

- For the children to have a positive image of themselves, as people created in the image of God.
- For the children to recognize the important people and events in their journey through life.
- To help the children to understand that their faith is part of this journey and that their preparation to meet Jesus through Holy Communion is the next stage.

I believe

I believe in God, the Father almighty, creator of heaven and earth.

SESSION 1

Biblical basis

Mark 10:13–14; Psalm 139:1, 3–5

Preparation and resources

1. Assemble a 'Ready Box' of the basic resources that you will need for every session. A suggested list is provided in chapter 5 on page 23.

2. Prepare a register containing the children's names, addresses, contact numbers and any other information about special needs or medical conditions. However small the group may be, this information should be immediately available in case of a child being taken ill or not turning up for a session.

3. Make a 'Path of life'. Have ready a long piece of wallpaper with a path drawn on it. At the beginning of the path, write 'Birth', then 'Baptism'. Towards the end, write 'First Holy Communion' and then draw an arrow marked 'Looking to the future'. Write above it, 'We have started our journey towards receiving Holy Communion.'

4. Prepare some graphics of a cradle, font, bread and wine or similar pictures.

Before you start

As the children arrive, give them each a small piece of paper. Ask them to draw a picture of themselves (it need only be a pin figure) and write their name under it. Be prepared with a drawing of yourself and your own memories to add to the discussion.

Teaching time (15 minutes)

Ask the children what is the earliest thing they can remember. For some it will be going to pre-school; for others it may be a baby brother or sister being born. A few children can remember as far back as being barely two years old, so don't be surprised by some of the answers. Then ask about something special that has happened to them—any very happy or sad events.

Explain that our life is like a journey which starts when we are born and is marked by all sorts of big events like going to school, happy ones like birthdays, and also sad ones like illness and loss. Our journey as

Christians began when we were baptized. (If you have children who have not been baptized as babies, add that they have begun the journey by asking to be baptized.) Today, we are starting to travel on the path that leads to meeting Jesus in Holy Communion.

Continue by asking the children who helps them with their path of life: people like parents, friends and teachers. Explain that Jesus is also with them and loves them.

Read one of the following Bible passages:

Some people brought their children to Jesus so that he could bless them by placing his hands on them. But his disciples told the people to stop bothering him. When Jesus saw this, he became angry and said, 'Let the children come to me! Don't try to stop them. People who are like these little children belong to the kingdom of God.'

MARK 10:13–14

You have looked deep into my heart, Lord, and you know all about me. You know when I am resting or when I am working, and from heaven you discover my thoughts. You notice everything I do and everywhere I go. Before I even speak a word, you know what I will say, and with your powerful arm you protect me from every side.

PSALM 139:1–5

Discuss the reading briefly. Help the children to understand that God is always near to us. Do the following activity.

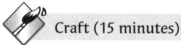 Craft (15 minutes)

Unroll or pin up the 'Path of life'. Let the children cut out the pictures that they have drawn of themselves and stick them on the path. Decorate it with the drawings or cut-out pictures of a cradle, font, bread and wine or similar images. Encourage the children to talk and ask questions about the pictures that you have provided as they are working.

 Focus on church

If this session has taken place on a Sunday, let the children help you to take the 'Path of life' into church and place it before the altar table at the offering of gifts. If it has been held on a weekday, end the session by taking the 'Path of life' into church or the worship area and having the worship time in there.

SESSION 2

Biblical basis

Genesis 1:1, 26–27a

Preparation and resources

You will need:
- ❖ The Ready Box
- ❖ The activity books
- ❖ Inkpad and magnifying glass, if you wish to do the craft activity

Before you start

As the children arrive, give them their activity books. Mark the register at the beginning of each session.

Teaching time (15 minutes)

Start by talking about the way the children started the last session by drawing pictures of themselves to go on the 'Path of life'. Look together at the first unit of the

Path of life

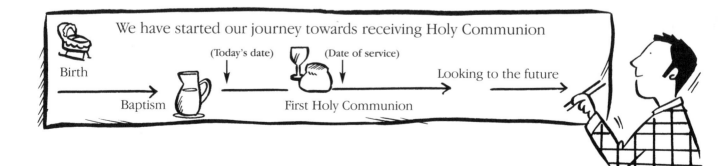
We have started our journey towards receiving Holy Communion

Birth — Baptism — (Today's date) — First Holy Communion — (Date of service) — Looking to the future

activity book. Explain that it is about who we are and how God has made each one of us to live in his world and be like him.

Explain that at the end of each unit the children will be asked to complete a section of the activity book at home. It will not be marked in the way that school work is, but they should try to do it well because, on the day that they first receive Holy Communion, they will offer their books as a gift to show God how much they love him. If they find anything difficult, they can ask their parents or leaders for help.

NB: Be aware that some children may find it hard to get help. See the section headed 'Using sponsors' in chapter 4, 'Involving the family'.

Go through the first task in the activity book so that each child is sure what he or she has to do.

Read the following Bible passage. If the children are not familiar with the creation story, try to make time to read it to them in full, maybe by using a simplified version from a book of Bible stories, or by telling it in your own words.

In the beginning God created the heavens and the earth… God said, 'Now we will make humans, and they will be like us. We will let them rule the fish, the birds, and all other living creatures.' So God created humans to be like himself; he made men and women.
GENESIS 1:1, 26–27a

Do at least one of the following activities to demonstrate that God has made each one of us to be different.

Game: Who am I? (10 minutes)

Sit in a circle. One person starts by saying three things about another person in the group: for example, 'He has dark hair and glasses and likes football. Who is he?' The others have to provide the answer. See that everyone is included.

Craft (10 minutes)

For this, you need an inkpad and some paper. Ask each child to make a thumb print by putting his or her thumb on the inkpad and then on the paper. Using the magnifying glass, show that each one of them has a different pattern.

Finding out (20 minutes)

Ask each of the children to say two things that they like about themselves. Show how they are all different. Ask the children to identify the different things that they are good at doing. Emphasize that they are all important. Being helpful or staying cheerful is just as valuable as being good at mathematics or football.

Worship

Always allow time to do the worship properly with no sense of rush. Set the atmosphere by stilling your voice and ensuring that everyone is sitting quietly before you start. The suggested prayers and a hymn or song will take between five and ten minutes.

Music

Can you count the stars? (SSL 25)
God knows me (CP 15)
It fell upon a summer day (SSL 31)
One more step along the world I go (CP 47; JP 188)
Think of a world without any flowers (SSL 15; CP 17)
Who put the colours in the rainbow? (JP 288; CP 12)

Prayer

Leader: We thank you, God, for making each one of us differently and starting us on the path of life.

All: Thank you, God.

Leader: Thank you for our families and all the people *(name some of them)* who care for us every day.

All: Thank you, God.

Leader: Thank you for all the special things that happen to us. *(If someone has a birthday or something else that is special at this time, use this as a chance to thank God for it.)*

All: Thank you, God.

Leader: We remember the times when we have been sad or angry. *(Pray for anyone who is in special need.)* We thank you for being with us and for anyone who has helped us.

All: Thank you, God.

Reproduced with permission from *Welcome to the Lord's Table* published by BRF 2006 (1 84101 504 0) www.barnabasinchurches.org.uk

Leader: We thank you for guiding us to start on this journey to meet Jesus in Holy Communion.

All: Thank you, God.

Leader: We pray for each other. *(At this point, the leader could name each person by turn or each child could name the person next to him or her.)* Thank you for... We pray to you in the name of Jesus our Lord. Amen

Tasks

1. Ask the children to complete Unit 1 of the activity book and bring it to the next session.
2. Ask the children to find out the date and place of their baptism. If anyone has not been baptized, make a note of this now.

Further action for leaders

❖ Check the attendance register of names, addresses and phone numbers. Keep it up to date.
❖ See that the 'Path of life' is displayed somewhere in church or at school for a few weeks so that the congregation is aware that the children have started on this part of their faith journey. Keep it safely as it will be needed for the final unit.
❖ Discuss how the first session has gone and if any of the children have special needs or problems.
❖ Find your own Christmas crib figures or arrange to borrow some from the church for the next session.

Reproduced with permission from *Welcome to the Lord's Table* published by BRF 2006 (1 84101 504 0) www.barnabasinchurches.org.uk

Jesus, our friend and brother

Aim

To teach that Jesus is God and also human.

Objectives

❖ For the children to recognize that Jesus was a real person, just as we are.
❖ To explain the part that Mary's faith and acceptance played in the birth of Jesus.
❖ To show that Jesus is always with us as our friend and brother.

I believe

I believe in Jesus Christ, his only Son... born of the Virgin Mary.

SESSION 1

Biblical basis

Luke 1:26–38; 2:1–20

Preparation and resources

1. Part of this session is about Mary being Jesus' mother and the fact that Jesus grew up in an ordinary family. Find out discreetly if any of the children do not live with both their natural parents or do not know who they are, or if a parent has died. Be prepared to affirm the role of the guardians and carers who act as parents for many children and the courage that is needed to bring up a child as a lone parent. It may be appropriate to explain that Joseph was Jesus' foster father and that tradition says that he was elderly and died when Jesus was young.

2. You will need a set of Christmas crib figures, displayed where the children can see and handle them.

Before you start

As the children arrive, let them ask any questions about the task they did in their activity books or finish anything that has not been completed.

Teaching time (20–30 minutes)

Start by looking at the section that the children have completed in their activity books. Try to find something positive to say about each one. Note any possible issues that may need to be followed up. Notice the sections, 'I live with...' and 'People who help me are...'

Explain that God calls us all to do different things for him. In our books, we have listed the people who look after us: parents, teachers, doctors, police and so on. Emphasize the importance of being a mother, or taking on the role of a mother, if any of the children are looked after by another family member. Ask the children what sort of things their mothers do for them.

Read the story of the annunciation, either from a children's Bible, or using the following retelling:

God sent the angel Gabriel to a town called Nazareth. He had a message for a young girl who was going to marry a man named Joseph, who was descended from the family of King David. The girl's name was Mary.

The angel came to her and said, 'Peace be with you! The Lord has blessed you!'

Mary was very worried by the angel's message and wondered what it meant.

The angel said, 'Don't be frightened, Mary. God is pleased with you. You are going to have a baby son and you will call him Jesus.'

Mary said to the angel, 'How can this happen?'

The angel answered, 'The Holy Spirit will come on you and God's power will rest on you. For this reason, the holy child will be called the Son of God.'

Mary said, 'I am the Lord's servant. I will do whatever he asks of me.'

BASED ON LUKE 1:26–38

Explain that the angel asked Mary to do a very difficult job. God was going to come in the person of Jesus and live as an ordinary person like us. He had asked Mary to be the mother of Jesus.

Read the last sentence again: 'Mary said, "I am the Lord's servant. I will do whatever he asks of me."' Ask the children, 'Did Mary say "yes" or "no"?' God does not force us to do things for him. He only asks us. Mary said 'yes' to him and became the mother of Jesus. (Responding to God's call is developed further in Units 5 and 10.)

Finding out (10 minutes)

Use the set of Christmas crib figures for a question-and-answer session to remind the children about the birth of Jesus (Luke 2:1–20).

• Ask the names of Mary and Joseph.
• Why is a donkey among the figures?
• Who are the other figures?
• Why are the shepherds there?
• Why are they kneeling? … and so on

Focus on church

Remind the children that we see a Christmas crib in church at Christmas time.

When we go into church for all of the Eucharist, we may sing the song of praise that the angels sang to the shepherds. It starts, 'Glory to God in the highest, and peace to his people on earth.'

Finish the session by singing a version of the Gloria or one of the annunciation songs listed in the section on music at the end of this unit.

SESSION 2

Biblical basis

Luke 2:42–50

Preparation and resources

You will need:
❖ The Ready Box
❖ Large sheets of brown paper from which to cut a tree outline
❖ Light-green paper leaves about 8cm x 12cm
  or
❖ A plant pot filled with earth, with a branch planted in it
❖ Outline pictures of biblical-style faces
❖ Thread
❖ Silver or gold spray paint (optional)

1. A large part of this session is taken up with making a Jesse tree. This is a pictorial representation of Jesus' family. It is based on Isaiah 11:1: 'Like a branch that sprouts from a stump, someone from David's family will some day be king.' (Jesse was the father of King David.) Advent is also a good time to make a Jesse tree as we remember that 'long ago in many ways and at many times God's prophets spoke his message to our ancestors' (Hebrews 1:1).

2. The two lists of Jesus' ancestors in the Gospels (Matthew 1:1–17 and Luke 3:23–38) are not identical and it is more helpful to take just the well-known names like Abraham, Isaac, Jesse and David. Only the fathers' names are listed but you could add famous women like Eve, Ruth and Mary. To emphasize Jesus' close family, you could include Zechariah and Elizabeth, the parents of John the

Baptist (Luke 1:5), and Mary's own parents, who, tradition says, were called Joachim and Anne. About a dozen names will be enough.

3. To save time, it is advisable to have the 'tree' prepared before the session. From sheets of brown paper, cut a simplified shape of a tree with bare branches. Fix it to the wall or mount it on a large sheet of paper that can then be hung on the wall. Alternatively, you could use a branch of a tree planted into an earth-filled pot.

Teaching time (10+ minutes)

Start by briefly reminding the children that, even though we hear all those stories about angels and wise men at Jesus' birth, he lived in a family just as we do. Jesus had a mother, grandparents and a family tree, which included kings, prophets and soldiers. Then use the main part of the session to make the Jesse tree.

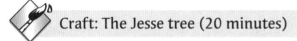
Craft: The Jesse tree (20 minutes)

First version

1. Make green paper leaves about 8cm x 12cm.
2. Spend a little time deciding which characters to have on the tree.
3. Using standard male and female face outlines, ask the children to make different characters by changing clothes, hair and so on.
4. Add the name of each character to the portrait.
5. Stick the face of each person on to a leaf. Fasten them on the tree.

Second version

1. If space is limited or it is easier to display work on a table, use a branch planted in a heavy, earth-filled plant pot.
2. To make it look festive, spray the branch with gold or silver paint.
3. Using standard male and female face outlines, ask the children to make different characters by changing clothes, hair and so on.
4. Add the name of each character to the portrait.
5. Tie them on to the branch with thread so that they look like Christmas tree decorations.

NB: If you make this version, save it to use again in Units 8 and 10.

Continue the story of Jesus' childhood by reminding the children that he did the same sort of things as children everywhere: he learned to read and write, asked questions and had adventures. When he was twelve, he had a big adventure when he went to the temple in Jerusalem. Read about Jesus in the temple, either from a children's Bible, or using the following retelling. Finish the session by sitting quietly.

When Jesus was twelve years old, he went with Mary and Joseph and their relatives and friends to the Passover festival in Jerusalem. When it was over, they all started back home, but Jesus stayed behind in Jerusalem. His parents did not realize this; they thought he was with other people in the group.

After they had travelled for a day, his parents started looking for him among their relatives and friends. They did not find him, so they went back to Jerusalem to look for him. They searched for three days and then they found him in the temple, sitting with the

Jewish teachers, listening to them and asking them questions. Everyone was amazed by his intelligent answers.

His parents were shocked when they found him. Mary said, 'Why did you do this to us? Your father and I have been really worried and looking everywhere for you.'

'Why did you have to look for me?' answered Jesus. 'Didn't you know that I would be in my Father's house?' They did not understand what he meant.

So Jesus went home to Nazareth. He already knew that God was his Father in a special way but he grew up with his parents, doing what they told him to do.

BASED ON LUKE 2:42–50

Worship

Music

Glory to God in the highest (JP 51)
Glory to God *(Peruvian Gloria)* (CHE 198)
Jesus, good above all other (CP 23)
The journey of life (SSL 28)
The Virgin Mary had a baby boy (JP 251)

Prayer

Leader: Thank you, God, for giving us Jesus to be a child like us, our friend and brother.

All: Lord, hear our prayer.

Leader: Thank you for choosing Mary to be Jesus' mother. Help us to say 'yes' when you ask us to serve you.

All: Lord, hear our prayer.

Leader: Jesus called the temple his Father's house. Help us to remember that you are our heavenly Father and that our church is your house.

All: Lord, hear our prayer.

Leader: Jesus asked questions from the teachers in the temple. Thank you for those who teach us about your love for us.

All: Lord, hear our prayer.

Leader: Mary and Joseph were sad when they lost Jesus and happy when they found him. Thank you for always being near us, when we are sad and when we are happy.

All: Lord, hear our prayer.

Leader: We make all of these prayers in the name of Jesus, our friend and brother. Amen

Tasks

1. The children should have found out the date of their baptism. Ask them to bring their baptismal certificates or written details next week if their parents have not already produced them. Note any children who have not been baptized.
2. Ask them to do the second task in their activity books.

Further action for leaders

❖ Display the Jesse tree in church. Save it to adapt for use in Units 8 and 9.
❖ Decide what action to take if any child has had difficulty in doing the work or has any other problem.
❖ Check that your vicar or minister knows about any child who has not been baptized so that he or she can discuss baptism with the parents.
❖ Arrange to collect the artefacts needed for the session on baptism. Find out if there will be a baptism that the children can see in the next few weeks.

Unit 3

God's family

 Aim

To teach that through baptism we are made part of God's family of Christians everywhere.

Objectives

❖ To recall that Jesus was baptized and that this was the beginning of his ministry.
❖ To explain that the children's parents and godparents started them on the Christian journey by having them baptized. Now they have chosen themselves to continue on that journey by being admitted to Holy Communion. (If you are preparing any children for baptism at the same time as admission to Holy Communion, remember to affirm this as something to look forward to, as they will make the baptismal vows for themselves.)
❖ To help the children to understand that, in baptism, we share in the death and resurrection of Jesus.
❖ To discuss some of the symbols connected with baptism.

I believe

I believe in the holy catholic Church.

SESSION 1

Biblical basis

Mark 1:4, 9–11

Preparation and resources

You will need:
❖ A large bowl of water
❖ A baptismal shell if your church uses one
❖ A doll

Before you start

As the children arrive, ask them if they have noted the date and place of their baptism or brought their baptismal certificate. Note down the details. Any children who have not been baptized must be baptized before they can receive Holy Communion.

Teaching time (15 minutes)

Start by asking the children to look at the prayer at the end of the last task in the activity book. What did Jesus teach us to call God?

Read or say the Lord's Prayer together in the version that your church uses.

Point out that the book describes it as a 'family' prayer. We are all God's children and he loves each one of us. We became part of his family, the Church, by being baptized.

Read the Bible story using the following version or a children's Bible. Before you read the story, explain that this event happened when Jesus was about 30 years old. People were asking John to baptize them as a way of showing that they were sorry for things they had done wrong and wanted to make a fresh start. If you have included John the Baptist on your Jesse tree, remind the children that he was a relative of Jesus.

John the Baptist appeared in the desert and told everyone, 'Turn back to God and be baptized! Then your sins will be forgiven.' … About that time Jesus came from Nazareth in Galilee, and John baptized him in the River Jordan. As soon as Jesus came out of the water, he saw the sky open and the Holy Spirit coming down to him like a dove. A voice from heaven said, 'You are my own dear Son, and I am pleased with you.'

MARK 1:4, 9–11

Even though Jesus had not done anything wrong, he asked John to baptize him and, as he came up out of the water, God's Holy Spirit descended on him. God said to him, 'You are my own dear Son. I am pleased with you.' It was only after this that Jesus started telling people about God and his love for us.

When we are baptized, we become part of God's family, the Church. Some people are baptized when they are babies; others wait until they are older or grown up. If we are baptized as babies, our parents promise to bring us up to know about God and to love him.

If any children are preparing to be baptized, point out that they are able to make the promises for themselves.

Drama (15 minutes)

NB: This activity may be left out if the children can be present at a real baptism instead.

Using the bowl of water and the doll, show how a baby is baptized. Gently pour the water over the doll's head three times, saying the words, '*(Name)*, I baptize you in the name of the Father and of the Son and of the Holy Spirit.' If there is time, you could get the children to choose a name for the 'baby' and act out the roles of the parents and godparents. Compare the act of baptism with a baby being bathed. Explain that the early Christians were baptized in the same way that Jesus was, by being totally immersed in the water. Some Christians today also choose to be baptized in this way.

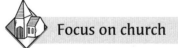

Focus on church

Find out if there is an opportunity to see someone being baptized. If there is not, show the children the font or baptistry when you next go into church. In some churches it is by the door to symbolize the newly baptized person's entry into the family of the Church; in others it is near the altar table and pulpit so that the sacrament is administered in full view of the whole congregation.

SESSION 2

✝ Biblical basis

Psalm 1:2–3; Isaiah 43:1

Preparation and resources

You will need:
- ❖ A bowl of water
- ❖ A cross
- ❖ Two plants, one dried up and the other growing
- ❖ A candle
- ❖ Matches
- ❖ Small mirrors

Teaching time (10 minutes)

Sit the children in a group with the bowl of water, the cross and the candle clearly visible. Talk about the symbols used in baptism.

Water

Ask the children how the water was used when they acted out a baptism in the last session (or watched a baptism in church). Then ask them to name ways in which we all need water: for drinking, washing, and making things grow are the most obvious.

Show them the two plants. They should grasp easily that one has not grown because it has not been watered. Explain that nothing can live without water. Some of the older children may have seen pictures on television of parts of the world where people are ill or even dying because of lack of water. The water used in baptism does not just wash away our sins (the things we do wrong), but it gives us new life, like water restoring a dried-up plant.

Read the following Bible passage:

The Law of the Lord makes (people) happy, and they think about it day and night. They are like trees growing beside a stream, trees that produce fruit in season and always have leaves.
PSALM 1:2–3

Remind the children that Jesus died on the cross for us and then came to life again. Our baptism links us with his death and resurrection. In the water of baptism, we die to our sins and share in his new risen life.

Our names

When we were baptized, the priest or minister used our names. This is to show that God knows each one of us individually and calls us by our names: our Christian names.

I have called you by name; now you belong to me.
ISAIAH 43:1

The cross

Make the sign of the cross on someone's forehead with your thumb. Talk about why it is important. Where do we see the cross displayed? Does anyone have one on the front of a prayer book, or wear one? At a baptism, the priest or minister signs the candidate with the sign of the cross and says, 'Christ claims you for his own. Receive the sign of his cross' (*Common Worship, Holy Baptism*, CHP, 2000). The idea of the sign of the cross as a sign of belonging to Jesus will be discussed in Unit 5.

Candle

Light the candle. Say together the words, 'You have received the light of Christ; walk in this light all the days of your life. Shine as a light in the world to the glory of God the Father' (*Common Worship, Holy Baptism*, CHP 2000).

Explain that baptism is a new beginning. We have come out of the darkness of sin and into the light of new life in Jesus.

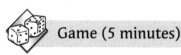

Game (5 minutes)

Using the lighted candle and mirrors, let the children 'catch' the candlelight in a mirror and reflect it around the room.

NB: Do not let the children touch the candles, or allow anyone to reflect the light across other people's eyes, as this can be dangerous. Encourage them to direct the mirrors so that the light shines in any dark corners and to notice how the single candle makes far more light when reflected in the mirrors. So it is with us. We can reflect Jesus' light in the world by the way that we live.

Prayer

Finish the session by sitting quietly in a circle with the water, the cross and the lighted candle as focal points. Say the 'family' prayer, the Lord's Prayer, while looking at the focal objects, and sing one of the suggested hymns or songs.

Music

From the darkness came light (CP 29)
God knows me *(There are hundreds of sparrows)* (CP 15; JP 246)
I'm special because God has loved me (JP 106)
Jesus bids us shine with a pure, clear light (JP 128)
Keep me shining, Lord (JP 147)
This little light of mine (JP 258; CHE 736)
Water of life *(Have you heard the raindrops)* (CP 2)

Tasks

1. Ask the children to complete the third task in their activity books.
2. Send home a note with the date when the children will be presented with their Bibles at the Sunday service.

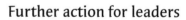

Further action for leaders

❖ Give your priest or minister the details of the children's baptisms that have been supplied, and arrange for follow-up if information is missing or if any child is uncertain about whether or not he or she has been baptized.
❖ Check that the Bibles and bookplates for presentation after Unit 4 have been purchased.

Unit 4

God's storybook

🎯 Aim

To discover the importance of the Bible.

⚠️ Objectives

❖ For the children to see the Bible as the story of God's saving grace and the good news of Jesus Christ. That story still continues today.
❖ To show the importance of the Bible in our personal lives and in our corporate worship.
❖ To introduce various ways of reading the Bible.

📜 I believe: the great commandment

You must love the Lord your God with all your heart, soul, mind, and strength... Love others as much as you love yourself (Mark 12:30–31).

SESSION 1

📖 Biblical basis

Luke 10:25–37

Preparation and resources

1. Assemble a few well-known children's books of different kinds: fiction, biography, poetry, music, history and so on. Include one with rules or laws in it, such as a Brownie or Cub handbook. Have a few DVDs or videos as well.

2. You will need the Ready Box and an A4 or A3 sheet with a Bible text for each child. There are examples on pages 88–90.

Before you start

Have some simple Bible stories around for the children to look at, or a biblical video or DVD to watch as they assemble. Include the children's Bible that you usually use, and some of the illustrated versions of single stories. Remember that some children in your group may find reading difficult, while others will be fluent readers. Be sensitive to this by incorporating other storytelling resources such as DVDs and videos. See that everyone is involved in some way if you do the drama activity.

Teaching time: Part 1 (15+ minutes)

Start the session by showing the children the various books that you had laid out and ask them if they know or can guess what each one is about. Point out that they are all different kinds of stories or information. We read some of them at school to find out about things; others are stories that we read at home or books about our hobbies or interests. Make sure you mention the book that contains rules or laws. Some of us enjoy reading books; others prefer to watch television, DVDs or videos or may get information from computers.

Explain that the Bible is not just a book, but a collection of books (sometimes called the scriptures). It tells us what God is like, and how he loves us and wants us to love him and each other. It is in two main parts. The Old Testament is about people who lived long before Jesus was born. It tells us about their friendship with God. The New Testament includes stories about Jesus and the things that he did and taught us. The Bible is like the collection of books we have been looking at, in that it contains stories, poems, history, letters, laws and rules, wise sayings called proverbs, songs, good news and stories about people who taught others about God.

Read the retelling of the Bible story below or use a version from a children's Bible. Introduce the story by explaining that people often went to Jesus to ask him questions about God, in the same way that we would ask our teachers or maybe our minister or priest. Jesus often answered by using words from the Old Testament or by telling stories.

A young man asked Jesus, 'Teacher, what must I do to have eternal life?'

Jesus answered him, 'What do the scriptures say?'

The man answered, 'Love the Lord your God and love your neighbours as much as you love yourself.'

'You are right,' Jesus replied; 'do this and you will have eternal life.'

The young man asked Jesus, 'Who are my neighbours?'

Jesus answered, 'There was once a man who was going down from Jerusalem to Jericho when robbers attacked him and grabbed everything he had. They beat him up and ran off, leaving him half dead.

'A priest happened to be going down the same road. But when he saw the man, he walked by on the other side. Later, a temple helper (a Levite) came to the same place. But when he saw the man who had been beaten up, he also went by on the other side.

'A man from Samaria then came travelling along that road. When he saw the man, he felt sorry for him and went to help him. He poured olive oil and wine on his wounds and bandaged them. Then he put the man on his own donkey and took him to an inn, where he could look after him. The next day he gave the innkeeper two silver coins and said, "Please take care of this man. If you spend any more, I will pay you when I return."'

Then Jesus asked, 'Which of these three acted like a neighbour towards the man attacked by the robbers?'

The man answered, 'The one who was

kind to him.'

Jesus replied, 'You go, then, and do the same.'

BASED ON LUKE 10:25–38

Explain that when the young man asked Jesus the question, 'What must I do to have eternal life?' Jesus did not make up his own answer. He replied with another question: 'What do the scriptures say?'

In the Bible we can find the answers to the way God wants us to live and love him and each other. Sometimes what we read is easy to understand; sometimes it makes us want to ask more questions. The young man already knew the answer. The Bible said, 'Love the Lord your God and love your neighbour as much as you love yourself.' But the young man wanted to know more. He asked Jesus, 'Who are my neighbours?'

Then Jesus told a story to show the young man that he should love anyone who was in need, not just his friends and family. The man from Samaria was a foreigner whom the Jewish people instinctively did not like, but he helped the man who had been attacked while other people ignored him.

When we read the stories that Jesus told or the wonderful things he did, such as healing people, we can get to know God better and learn what sort of people he wants us to be. Ask the children which Bible stories about Jesus they can remember.

Craft: Bible posters (20 minutes)

Give each child a poster to colour, containing one of the Bible verses overleaf. Photocopy the posters on pages 88–90, or draw your own. Use A3-size posters if you want to make them into banners in your next session.

Love the Lord your God. Love your neighbours as much as you love yourself.

LUKE 10:27

Your word is a lamp that gives light wherever I walk.

PSALM 119:105

If you keep on obeying what I have said, you truly are my disciples.

JOHN 8:31

SESSION 2

Biblical basis

Luke 10:25–37; Mark 12:29–31

Preparation and resources

You will need
- ❖ The Ready Box.

For each banner in the banner-making activity, you will also need:
- ❖ A3 posters which the children have made and coloured
- ❖ Two garden canes, one about 30cm long and one at least 60cm long
- ❖ Masking tape
- ❖ Cardboard (optional)

You will also need a Bible for each child for the 'Finding out' activity.

Teaching time (10 minutes)

Start the session by reminding the children about the way that we find out about God through the stories in the Bible. Take it a step further by explaining that when we hear or read the Bible, we hear God speaking to us through the people who wrote it. When the Bible is read in church, the person reading it often finishes by saying, 'This is the word of the Lord' or 'May God bless this reading of his word'. The stories about Jesus are especially important because they are the words he spoke and the things that he did. These stories are

called the Gospels. Gospel means 'good news'.
Do at least one of the following activities.

Craft: Banner making (20 minutes)

This is an extension of the poster making in the previous session.

1. If you want the posters to be less flimsy, you can mount them on card, but this is not essential.
2. Lay the short garden cane across the back of the poster about halfway up. Fasten it securely with masking tape.
3. Lay the long cane down the length of the poster to make a vertical support and handhold. Fasten it in several places with masking tape.
4. Stronger versions can be made in the same way, using A2-sized card with a collage to give more depth and texture than paint or felt-tipped pens.

Drama (20 minutes)
plus rehearsal time if to be acted in church

Act out the story of the good Samaritan. If there is not time or an opportunity to act it in church, read it in parts or let a couple of leaders read it while the children mime the story.

> **CAST**
> - ❖ Ben
> - ❖ Jesus
> - ❖ Dan (non-speaking)
> - ❖ A priest
> - ❖ Lee Vite
> - ❖ Sam Aritan
> - ❖ Muggers (non-speaking)

If the drama is acted in church, start with Ben and Jesus standing in the centre, then moving to the side to allow the action to take place.

Ben   Jesus, I've been thinking...

Jesus   That sounds like hard work! What have you been thinking about?

Ben   Well, it is a bit tricky. What must I do to get eternal life?

Jesus   Oh Ben, you can work that out for yourself! What does the Bible say?

Ben	Love the Lord your God and love your neighbour as much as you love yourself. That's easy!
Jesus	That's right. So, what's your problem?
Ben	Well, Jesus, I am not sure who my neighbours are.
Jesus	Oh, I see. Let me tell you a story. *(Pause)* There was once a man who was going down from Jerusalem to Jericho when robbers attacked him, grabbed everything he had and beat him up, leaving him half dead.

Enter Dan, wearing jeans and leather jacket, carrying rucksack, closely followed by the muggers. Mime beating up with lots of yells. The thieves snatch Dan's rucksack and jacket. Dan is left lying on the ground. Exit muggers.

Enter a priest. He stops and looks at Dan, but does not go too close to him.

Priest	Oh dear! He looks in a bit of a mess. But you never know with these young people. He's probably on drugs. *(Looks at his watch)* Anyway, I can't do anything now. I'm nearly late for the next service.

Priest exits.

Enter Lee Vite. He stops, goes up to Dan and bends down.

Lee Vite	Goodness, it's young Dan. Well, he always was mixing with the wrong sort of people, so I'm not surprised. I'd better not get involved or I might get beaten up too.

Exit Lee Vite in a hurry.

Enter Sam Aritan. He notices Dan, stops and hesitates. Dan groans.

Sam Aritan	Goodness, you are in a bad way. I can't just leave you like that. *(He bends over him and touches his head)* Oh, you're so cold. I'll cover you up with my coat while I get help. Trouble is, I don't live round here. *(He takes out a mobile phone)* 9, 9, 9… Yes, I need an ambulance quickly. A young man has been injured… I don't know exactly where I am. I'm a stranger. I'm in a place called Jericho Road. Good, thank you. *(He turns back to Dan)* The ambulance is on its way. I'll stay here and go to the hospital with you to see that you are looked after and have everything you need.

Ambulance siren noise. Sam Aritan helps Dan to get up and move away. Jesus and Ben walk towards the centre.

Jesus	Well, Ben, which one of those people was Dan's real neighbour?
Ben	I suppose it was the one who was kind to him.
Jesus	Exactly! Now, you go and do the same.

Finding out: for older children (15 minutes)

Find out if any of the children go to a library or if they use a library at school. Recall the first teaching session by reminding the children that the Bible is not just a book, but a whole collection of books, like a library. It contains stories about things Jesus said and did, which are called Gospels, and also stories about people such as Noah, Moses and Elijah. There are poems, letters and wise sayings as well as books about history and the law. Look at the index in your Bibles and see if you can identify what some of the books are about.

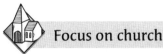 **Focus on church**

In some church services, we show how important the Gospel is by standing up when we hear it read. It may be read from a stand called a lectern or the book may

Reproduced with permission from *Welcome to the Lord's Table* published by BRF 2006 (1 84101 504 0) **www.barnabasinchurches.org.uk**

be carried, held up high, into the middle of the church or the pulpit, with two people carrying candles to remind us how Jesus' words are like light in our lives. In other churches, a large Bible is always displayed on the altar table, maybe with flowers, so that everyone can see it clearly. It does not matter which way is used in your church. What matters is for the children to know that the Bible is important and to recognize some of the ways that we show it.

Ask the children where the Bible is kept in your church. From where is it read? Do we do anything special when the reading is the Gospel, a story about Jesus? Ask them to notice this next time they are in church. Tell them that next Sunday (or on...) they are going to celebrate learning about God's story by being given their own Bible (or New Testament) in church. (See 'Marking the Journey', pages 41–43, for details.)

Further action for leaders

❖ Keep the posters or banners to decorate the church. The children could also act the story of the good Samaritan as a dramatized Gospel reading.
❖ Liaise with whoever is leading the service when the children are presented with their Bibles, especially if the children are to be involved in a procession with their banners, reading or acting the Gospel.
❖ Ensure that there is publicity about the service on the notice sheet.

Worship

Prayer

Thank you, God, for giving us the story of your love for us through the Bible. Help us to hear your words, learn from them and grow to be more like Jesus. Amen

Music

Cross over the road (CP 70)
Heavenly Father, may thy blessing (CP 62)
Make the book live to me (JP 63)
Tell me the stories of Jesus (JP 228)
When Jesus walked in Galilee (CP 25)

Tasks

1. Give the children a note to take home about the Bibles being presented in church, so that their families can be there to support them.
2. Ask them to bring their new Bibles to future sessions.
3. Complete Unit 4 in the activity book.
4. Ask the children if they have some books of Bible stories at home, or lend one of those on display at the beginning of the session. Encourage them to read it or get someone to read it to them before the next session. With children of nine years or over, it may be possible gently to encourage regular Bible reading.

Welcome and presentation of Bibles

⌖ Aim

For the worshipping community to welcome the children who have started on the stage of their Christian journey that leads to receiving Holy Communion.

⚠ Objectives

❖ To mark the children's starting their preparation course by presenting them with Bibles on behalf of the congregation.
❖ To reinforce the importance of the Bible in a Christian's personal life and in public worship.
❖ To emphasize the support of the whole worshipping community for the children and their families.

This ceremony should take place during the Sunday morning service, which, if possible, should be a service of Holy Communion. Ideally, the service should be soon after the children have studied Unit 4, 'God's storybook', so that it reinforces what has been learnt as well as giving the congregation an opportunity to welcome the children at an early stage of the preparation course. If the children are used to being in church and taking part in the worship, there will only be need for rehearsal if any of them are actively involved in the service.

If the children are being prepared as part of their school community, the 'Marking the journey' ceremonies should take place during a school service, preferably a Eucharist. If the school celebrates Holy Communion only occasionally, 'Marking the journey' should take place during a special act of worship.

Preparation

• Decorate the church with the 'Path of life' made during the first session, and the posters made as part of Unit 4. If they have been made into banners, the service could start with the children processing in with them and then displaying them near to the front or around the altar table.

• Arrange for the children to sit in the front row with their parents and sponsors sitting immediately behind them. See that other children from the Junior Church (or the children's classmates) are present to support their friends.

• Try to involve the children in the service by asking them to read the lessons, perform a dramatized reading such as the version of the good Samaritan in Unit 4, or lead some music. .

• See that the children who are reading get an opportunity to practise coming forward to the lectern or pulpit, reading out loud and moving back to their seat. Give the text to them in plenty of time so that they can take it home to practise beforehand.

• Any drama or music should always be rehearsed in the church with someone seated near the back to check that the performers can be both seen and heard.

• See that the Bibles or New Testaments have been purchased. It adds to the feeling of the community's support if they are inscribed with a simple message such as:

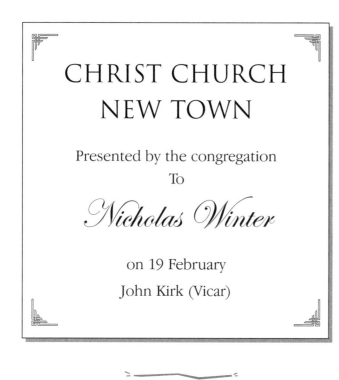

CHRIST CHURCH NEW TOWN

Presented by the congregation

To

Nicholas Winter

on 19 February

John Kirk (Vicar)

THE SERVICE

Bible readings

If your church uses a Lectionary, the readings will have been prescribed. However, it is important to bear in mind that there will be young families and children present, so a reading may need to be shortened or even omitted. In churches that choose their own themes, those that focus on being chosen or called would be appropriate and would anticipate the next unit in the course, 'Jesus' friends', which explores the meaning and responsibilities of discipleship. Another theme to consider might be God speaking to us through his word.

Possible Old Testament readings would be:

1 Samuel 3:1–10: The child Samuel responds to God's call
Isaiah 6:1–8: Isaiah's vision
Psalm 119:97–106: Love for the word of the Lord

Possible New Testament readings would be:

Mark 1:16–20: Jesus chooses four fishermen (used in Unit 5, 'Jesus' friends')
John 15:1–5: 'I am the vine, and you are the branches' (used in Unit 10, 'Let's share a meal')
Luke 4:16–21: 'What you have just heard me read has come true today'
Luke 10.25-37: 'What is written in the scriptures?' The good Samaritan (used in Unit 4, 'God's storybook')

Prayers

The families of the candidates or the children themselves could be involved with the prayers. They can each be given their prayer on a card or asked to write their own on a particular subject. Topics similar to those to be used in Unit 6 would form a suitable basis: the Church, the world, the locality, those in need, and those who are unwell or who are dying. The prayers should include asking God's blessing on the preparation course, its leaders, the children by name and their families.

Music

Any of the hymns and songs listed in Units 4 and 5 could be used. Also consider the following, which are in general use as well as being connected with the readings:

Follow me (CHE 175)
Mark 1:16–20

God's Spirit is in my heart (CHE 227)
Luke 4:16–21

Here I am, Lord (CHE 285)
Isaiah 6:1–8

Hushed was the evening hymn (JP 85)
1 Samuel 3:1–10

I am the vine (CHE 273)
John 15:1–5

I will make you fishers of men (JP 123)
Mark 1:16–20

Lord, thy Word abideth (CHE 390)
Psalm 119

When I needed a neighbour (CHE 800; JP275)
Luke 10:25–37

The welcome and presentation

If the theme of the service is announced at the beginning, or if there are notices, this is a good time to say that part of the service will include welcoming the children who have started the preparation course and presenting them with Bibles. The best place for the presentation would be after the scripture readings or the sermon.

The following ceremony is just a suggestion. Feel free to use your own ideas that may be more in keeping with the tradition of your church.

Introduction to the service

The priest or minister introduces the service:

We meet today as God's family, gathered round his table to share in the meal that the Lord gave us. Today's Bible readings remind us that Jesus called his disciples to follow him. He calls us in the same way and gives us the strength to respond, 'Here I am, Lord, send me.' It is a great pleasure to welcome the children with their families who have answered Jesus' call by starting to prepare to receive Holy Communion. Later in the service we will be praying for them and showing our support and friendship by presenting them with Bibles.

After the scripture readings or sermon

The children and their parents or sponsors stand at the front. The priest or minister addresses the people:

Dear friends, we are very happy to welcome these children. They have started on the part of their Christian journey that leads to meeting Jesus in the receiving of Holy Communion. They started this journey when they were baptized and made members of Christ's family. During the next few months, with their leaders and parents, they will continue to learn about loving and following the Lord Jesus as his disciples.

The priest or minister addresses the children by their names:

N and N, do you want to grow in love for the Lord Jesus and meet him in Holy Communion?

The children reply together:

We do.

The priest or minister then addresses those who are teaching the children:

Parents, sponsors and leaders, will you help these children along this stage of their Christian journey?

They reply together:

We will.

The priest or minister then addresses the whole congregation:

Dear friends, will you all support these children, their families and leaders with your prayers and your friendship?

They reply together:

We will.

The priest or minister then addresses the children by their names:

N and N, we rejoice that you are taking this step forward on your Christian journey. As a token of our love and support, we present each of you with a Bible, the word of the Lord, to be your light and your guide. May God bless you as you continue with us on your journey of faith.

The children and their parents and sponsors sit down and the service continues as usual.

Reproduced with permission from *Welcome to the Lord's Table* published by BRF 2006 (1 84101 504 0) www.barnabasinchurches.org.uk

Unit 5

Jesus' friends

Aim

To discover the meaning and responsibilities of discipleship.

Objectives

❖ To develop the idea of belonging to Jesus through our baptism.
❖ To recall the choosing of the first disciples.
❖ To use the model of the summary of the Law to explore ways in which we can follow Jesus.
❖ To touch upon the concept of the communion of saints.

I believe

I believe in the communion of saints.

You must love the Lord your God with all your heart, soul, mind, and strength… Love others as much as you love yourself (Mark 12:30–31).

SESSION 1

Biblical basis

1 Peter 2:17

Preparation and resources

1. Collect some badges connected with school, uniformed organizations, football teams and so on.

Make sure that you know a little about the meaning behind the design of each one.

2. Have the badges displayed so that the children can look at them and identify to which organizations they belong.

3. You will need the Ready Box and an outline of a shield for each child. This may be copied from the activity book.

Before you start

As the children arrive, compliment them on the way that the presentation of Bibles went on the previous Sunday, or whenever it happened. If children were absent, use this opportunity to give them their Bibles. Try to steer the thin line between regretting that those children missed the celebration and being proscriptive about their absence. Ask them to bring their Bibles to the next session. Look at the activity books. Try to say something encouraging about each one.

Teaching time (20 minutes)

Start by asking the children about the badges. As well as getting the name of the organization, see if you can unpack a little of the symbolism behind them. For example, Brownie and Cub Scout badges represent the threefold promise; school badges are usually linked to the name of the school or locality; football club badges often illustrate their history or name.

Ask why we wear badges and draw out that it is either because we belong to the particular school or club, or because we support it. Belonging to a particular school or organization means that there are certain things we are expected to do. When we are in public, our particular school or club is judged by the way we behave. (The children should all be familiar

44

with this idea and will probably tell you about it without any prompting.)

Refer to the session about baptism (Unit 3). When we were baptized, we were given a badge. It was the sign of the cross on our foreheads. Draw out who we belong to, who we support because we wear this badge. It cannot be seen, although some of us may wear a cross, but people will know that we are Christians—followers of Christ—and will form their opinions by the way we behave.

Read the Bible passage below. Remind the children that the Bible consists of lots of books of different kinds. Some of them were letters that Jesus' friends wrote to the early Christians to teach them more about Jesus and how his followers should behave. This is part of what Peter, one of Jesus' closest friends, wrote to a group of Christians:

Respect everyone and show special love for God's people. Honour God and respect the Emperor.
1 PETER 2:17

Explain briefly that Peter is not just telling people to love God and the people who are close to us, but to treat everyone properly and to respect people who are in authority and make our laws.

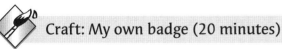
Craft: My own badge (20 minutes)

Give each child an outline of a shield with the cross in the centre. Either use the example in the activity book or draw your own.

Ask them to start to design a badge that says something about their lives. Use each quarter of the

shield to illustrate things about their lives: family, church, school, hobbies and interests. Explain that the cross in the centre holds all the different parts of their lives together.

NB: A few children do not enjoy drawing, or find it very difficult, so always allow the option of writing or sticking in pictures from magazines. Some may be confident enough to do the work straight into their books, while others may wish to make a rough plan and finish the work at home.

SESSION 2

📖 Biblical basis
Mark 1:16–20; Luke 10:27

Preparation and resources

Have some spare Bibles ready in case any of the children have forgotten theirs.

Teaching time (15 minutes)

Take a few minutes to help the children to find their way around their new Bibles. Show them the division between the Old and New Testaments. Find the four Gospels at the beginning of the New Testament and remind the children that they tell us the things that Jesus said and did, as well as the stories he told us to show what God was like. Help them to find the beginning of Mark's Gospel and today's story.

Read the story of Jesus choosing his first disciples, using the version below or a children's story Bible. To introduce the story, remind the children that badges show that people belong to or follow something. The sign of the cross made at our baptism shows that we belong to Jesus and follow him. Now we are going to find out about the first people who followed Jesus.

As Jesus was walking along the shore of Lake Galilee, he saw Simon and his brother Andrew. They were fishermen and were casting their nets into the lake. Jesus said to them, 'Come with me! I will teach you how to bring in people instead of fish.' At once the two brothers dropped their nets and went with him.

Jesus walked on and soon saw James and John, the sons of Zebedee. They were in a boat, mending

their nets. At once Jesus asked them to come with him. They left their father in the boat with the hired workers and went with him.

MARK 1:16–20

Point out that Jesus had lots of friends, both men and women, but that these four men were the first of twelve disciples whom he used to help him to tell people the good news of God's promises for his people. Remind the children that Jesus gave Simon the name of Peter, whose letter we read a little of in the previous session. Peter travelled all over the known world teaching about Jesus.

Finding out (15 minutes)

- Who is your best friend?
- Why is he or she special?
- What sort of things do you do together?
- How do you try to be a good friend?

Jesus is our friend. We are close to him when we pray or read about him in the Bible and when we meet other people who are trying to follow him.

Being a follower of Jesus affects all sorts of things that we say and do. It can be summed up in what is known as the Summary of the Law: 'Love the Lord your God with all your heart, soul, strength, and mind... Love your neighbours as much as you love yourself' (Luke 10:27).

- Can anyone remember where they have heard that before?
- How did the good Samaritan show he loved his neighbour?
- Can you think of ways in which you can try to do this?

Game (5 minutes)

Finish the session with a few minutes of fun by playing a 'following' game, such as 'Simon says' or 'Follow my leader'.

Focus on church (10 minutes)

Remind the children that we are not alone as we try to follow Jesus. We have the example of people who have responded to God's call and shown people what Jesus is like. We call them saints. Some are alive today. Others are in heaven with God and, whenever we worship him, we are joining with their praises. There are several ways in which we are reminded of this when we are in church. Talk to the children about any of the following ways that they will have experienced in your church:

- In the Apostles' Creed, we say, 'I believe in the communion of saints', the community of all believers, both here on earth and in heaven.
- At the Eucharist, we worship God: 'With angels and archangels and with all the company of heaven, we proclaim your great and glorious name, for ever praising you and saying, 'Holy, holy, holy Lord...' (*Common Worship, Holy Communion, Order 1*)
- Stained-glass windows often have pictures of saints that provide a pictorial reminder that they are worshipping God with us.
- Hymns such as 'Holy, holy, holy, Lord God almighty' (verse 2), 'For all the saints' (verse 4) and 'Let saints on earth together sing' refer to the communion of saints.

Worship

Music

A man for all the people (CP 27)
I have decided to follow Jesus (JP 98)
My faith, it is an oaken staff (CP 46)
The journey of life (SSL 28; CP 45)
Think, think on these things (SSL 38)
We are climbing Jesus' ladder (CP 49)

Prayer

Leader: Jesus, we thank you for calling us to be your friends and followers. Help us to follow you by loving you and our neighbour.

All: Lord, hear our prayer.

Leader: Thank you for letting us meet you in our prayers, reading the Bible and in other people.

All: Lord, hear our prayer.

Leader: Thank you for our friends and people who care for us. Help us to be good friends to others too.

All: Lord, hear our prayer.

Leader: Thank you for the saints who have followed you and are now close to you in heaven.

All: Lord, hear our prayer.

Leader: You taught your friends how to pray. So we say together, Our Father...

Tasks

1. Ask the children to think about ways in which they can be good followers of Jesus.
2. See that they take home the rough plans of their shields so that they can complete them in their activity books, with the work for Unit 5.

Further action for leaders

Think if, from the discussion, any children appear to be lonely or friendless. See if you can do anything to steer them gently towards the company of other children.

Reproduced with permission from *Welcome to the Lord's Table* published by BRF 2006 (1 84101 504 0) www.barnabasinchurches.org.uk

Thank you; please

Aim

To help the children to develop their relationship with God through worship and prayer.

Objectives

❖ To explore the idea of spiritual experience.
❖ To understand that God is active in our lives through prayer.
❖ To discuss the use of intercession.

I believe

I believe in Jesus Christ, his only Son, our Lord.

SESSION 1

Biblical basis

Mark 9:2–5, 7–8

Preparation and resources

You will need:
❖ The Ready Box
❖ CD or tape of quiet music and means to play it
❖ Candle or other focal points for prayer: for example, a cross, or picture
❖ A few items that show the glory of God by their beauty, such as flowers, pebbles or glass beads

1. Prepare the frieze illustrated on pages 50–51 by drawing the words 'This is my own dear Son—listen to him!' in bubble writing, putting each word on a separate piece of paper for colouring in.

3. Practise reading the Bible passage over the sound of the music. It is not difficult, but speed and timing are important.

4. As this unit is about prayer, there is worship in both sessions. Allow ample time for it, as it illustrates the teaching in the unit. There is also a small task connected with worship for the children to do before the second session. Keep the timing flexible by doing the craft activity in any spare time across both sessions.

Before you start

As the children arrive, give each child a piece of paper with a word on it to start colouring in for the frieze. Use the opportunity to look at the activity books to check that all the work has been completed.

Teaching time (15 minutes)

Start by reminding the children that, even though Jesus was the Son of God, he looked just like any other person. Last week, we learned that Jesus was a teacher who travelled about with his special friends and followers—his disciples. Sometimes he was teaching huge crowds; other times, he wanted to be with a few friends. Today's story tells us about a time when some of the disciples saw Jesus as the Son of God with the glory of God shining through him.

Read the Bible passage from either the following version or a children's Bible. Before you read it, ask the children to sit still while you play some quiet music to set the atmosphere. Suggested music is listed on page 50, but any quiet, atmospheric music will do. Read the story of the transfiguration over the music and fade it out after you have finished.

Jesus took Peter, James, and John with him. They went up a high mountain, where they could be alone. There in front of the disciples, Jesus was completely changed. And his clothes became much whiter than any bleach on earth could make them. Then Moses and Elijah were there talking with Jesus.

Peter said to Jesus, 'Teacher, it is good for us to be here! Let us make three shelters, one for you, one for Moses, and one for Elijah.' …

The shadow of a cloud passed over and covered them. From the cloud a voice said, 'This is my Son, and I love him. Listen to what he says!' At once the disciples looked around, but they only saw Jesus.
MARK 9:2–5, 7–8

Explain that Jesus showed his glory, the glory of God, and for a moment his friends saw him as he really was. The world is full of God's glory. We have glimpses of it in beautiful things like flowers, snowflakes and rainbows, in the world he created and in people we love. Refer back to the first unit in the activity books: 'God made the universe, and he saw it was good.'

Do one of the following 'Finding out' activities, choosing the one that is more appropriate for your group. Bear in mind the children's backgrounds, their experience of worship and prayer, as well as their ages.

49

Finding out: the wonder of creation (15 minutes)

Encourage the children to talk about special times when they have had a glimpse of God's glory in the world. It may be something as unusual and beautiful as a rainbow or something simpler, like seeing the sun set behind tall buildings or feeling its warmth.

These moments can lead us towards being aware that we are in the presence of God, and worshipping him. They may be linked to particular places or occasions, in church, in the open air, or when something very special has happened. Most of the time, life is rather ordinary, and it is not easy to remember that God is with us. We can use things to help us, like sitting quietly before we pray, listening to music, or looking at a cross or a lighted candle.

Encourage the children to offer comments about praying. Be willing to share your own experiences of prayer, including the difficulties and times that you slip up. Remind the children what the disciples heard: 'This is my own dear Son—listen to him!' God told the disciples who Jesus was and ordered them to listen to him. When we pray, we need to listen to God as well as talking to him.

Finding out: Continuing the disciples' experience (15 minutes)

How do you think the disciples must have felt when they saw God's glory shining through Jesus? Collect some of the words.

What did they begin to understand about Jesus? That he was not just a man, but was God. Before this time, they may have wondered who he was, but now they saw it for themselves. Explain that Peter wanted to make tents for Jesus, Moses and Elijah so that this wonderful vision would go on for ever. But life is not like that. We cannot contain this sort of experience of the presence of God. It is rather like getting glimpses of the sun on a cloudy day.

Encourage the children to talk about times when they have felt the presence of God, maybe when they are alone, in church, or on a Christian weekend or pilgrimage. It may also be in the open air, as happened to the disciples. Remind the children what the disciples heard: 'This is my own dear Son—listen to him!' God told the disciples who Jesus was and ordered them to listen to him. When we pray, we need to listen to God as well as talking to him. Invite the children to offer comments about praying. Be willing to share your own experiences of prayer, including the difficulties and times that you slip up.

Craft (if time allows)

Start to create a frieze with the words the disciples heard, that the children have been colouring: 'This is my own dear Son—listen to him!' Stick them on the frieze. This will be continued in the next session.

Worship

Music for listening

Use quiet, atmospheric music, which may include the following:
'Morning', *Peer Gynt Suite* (Grieg)
Canon (Pachelbel)

Music for singing

Be still and know that I am God (JP 22)
Father, we love you, we worship and adore you (JP 45)
I'm very glad of God (SSL 22; JP 107)
Peace, perfect peace (CP 53)

Prayer

Finish the session with a brief act of worship that sums up the session. Sit in a circle around a lighted candle and a few objects that remind us of the glory of God: flowers, glass crystals, shells or pretty pebbles. Recall the transfiguration story by listening to a few bars of the music again and than fading it out to create a silence.

Thank God for this time together and ask the children quietly if there is anything they want to thank God for, either by speaking aloud or in their thoughts. Sum it up by singing a simple worship song from the list.

Task

Ask each child to bring something that reminds them of the glory of God to decorate the frieze next time. It can be their own drawings, printed pictures or small items and may be connected with nature but also directly with worship: for example, candles or a cross.

Biblical basis

Luke 11:1–13

Preparation and resources

Have the frieze laid out for the children to complete.

You will need:
- ❖ The Ready Box
- ❖ A few pictures connected with worship for the frieze, including bread and wine
- ❖ Sheet of A2 or flip-chart paper
- ❖ Two shoe boxes or ice cream containers, one marked 'Thank you' and one marked 'Please'

Before you start

As the children arrive, ask them to complete the frieze by adding their items that remind them of the glory of God. Add your pictures connected with worship to the various creation items.

Teaching time (20 minutes)

When the frieze is complete, remind the children that the things they have put on it show the glory of God. We experience God's glory in nature and also in worship. Point out that some of the things that are there are also things that we need. For example, the sun gives light and warmth; honey comes from flowers; wool for clothes comes from sheep and so on. The bread we use in the Eucharist is also basic food. Without food and drink we would die.

Read the Bible passage from the following version or a children's Bible.

Jesus said, 'Suppose one of you goes to a friend in the middle of the night and says, "Let me borrow three loaves of bread. A friend of mine has dropped in, and I don't have a thing for him to eat." And suppose your friend answers, "Don't bother me! The door is bolted, and my children and I are in bed.

I cannot get up to give you something."

'He may not get up and give you the bread, just because you are his friend. But he will get up and give you as much as you need, simply because you are not ashamed to keep on asking.

'So I tell you to ask and you will receive, search and you will find, knock and the door will be opened for you. Everyone who asks will receive, everyone who searches will find, and the door will be opened for everyone who knocks. Which one of you fathers would give your hungry child a snake if the child asked for a fish? Which one of you would give your child a scorpion if the child asked for an egg? As bad as you are, you still know how to give good gifts to your children. But your heavenly Father is even more ready to give the Holy Spirit to anyone who asks.'

LUKE 11:5–13

Ask the children if they remember a time when they needed something and someone helped them. Remind the children of the story of the good Samaritan (Unit 4). Help them to imagine what it is like to be hurt or lonely, to be ill or hungry. Recall the summary of the Law: the second part says, 'Love your neighbours as much as you love yourself.'

Take a large sheet of paper and divide it into three columns and five lines. Help the children to identify one need in each of the places and see if there is anything they can do to help.

Place	Situation	Action
The world	Famine in Africa	Give money to an aid charity
Great Britain	Children with disabilities	Fund-raising activity
Care home for the elderly	Loneliness	Sing carols at Christmas
School	New child in the class	Ask him or her to join your group
Home	Relative who is in hospital	Visit or send a card

Talk a little about praying for people in need. Explain that when we pray for people we begin to see them as our neighbours and then want to help them. This is our way of sharing in God's work.

Do one of the following activities.

Drama (20 minutes)
plus rehearsal time if to be acted in church

Act out this short play, 'Unexpected Guests'. If time is limited or the group is small, read it through, doubling up some of the parts. If it is to be acted in church, use the pulpit for Joshua and Jessica's house and arrange an area with chairs at the opposite side of the church to be Andrew and Ellie's house. The airport will be at the entrance of the building as far away from the main action as is possible.

CAST	PROPS
❖ Andrew	❖ A ring of chairs to
❖ Jesus	make a house
❖ Ellie	❖ Suitcases
❖ Thomas	❖ A carrier bag
❖ Sophie	
❖ Joshua	
❖ Jessica	

Ellie is sitting in the house area near to the centre of the action. Joshua and Jessica are hiding on the floor of the pulpit. Thomas and Sophie are at the entrance. Jesus is standing or sitting by the lectern. Andrew walks up to Jesus.

Andrew Jesus?

Jesus Yes, Andrew.

Andrew You know John taught his disciples to pray. Will you teach us?

Jesus The best way to pray? Well, something like this. Remember, God is your Father so start by calling him that. Say, 'Our Father...'

Andrew Our Father...

Jesus *(Continues with the Lord's Prayer until...)* 'Give us today our daily bread...'

Andrew Hang on a minute. I don't want to argue, and it's really good so far, but you can't expect God to give you daily bread just like that.

Jesus Why not?

Andrew Well, you know, it doesn't just happen. We were fishermen before

	we met you and sometimes we would work all night and catch hardly anything. And you know the story about the famine that sent our ancestors off to Egypt. They ended up as slaves.
Jesus	Oh, I see! You're in one of your worrying moods! How many times have I told you not to worry about the future? Look, Andrew, just suppose that you are at home one evening and there is a knock on the door.

Andrew joins Ellie. They appear to talk or read magazines.

Enter the travellers, carrying suitcases down the nave from the back of the church. They arrive at the house and mime knocking. Ellie opens the door.

Ellie	Good heavens. Thomas and Sophie! We weren't expecting you until tomorrow!
Sophie	We got an earlier flight. We tried to phone you from the airport but couldn't get a signal so we just came straight here.
Andrew	Well, it's a wonderful surprise. But you must be tired out and hungry. I'll get you something to eat while Ellie makes up your beds.
Thomas	That sounds great!
Ellie	*(Takes Andrew aside)* Andy, have you forgotten? You didn't get the shopping after work. We've got hardly anything to eat.
Andrew	Right, you keep them talking and I'll nip next door and borrow a loaf and some eggs. We can have omelettes.

Ellie gets Thomas and Sophie to sit down. They mime talking. Andrew goes to stand beneath the pulpit.

Andrew	Joshua! Jessica!

Jessica	*(Puts head over pulpit)* What do you want?
Andrew	Our friends have turned up from Australia and we are a bit low on food. Can you help us out?
Jessica	You've got a cheek! Do you know what time it is?
Andrew	Oh, come on, do us a favour. What are friends for?
Joshua	*(Joins Jessica)* Come off it, Andy, it's gone midnight and we've locked up. Get lost, there's a good mate, or you'll wake up the children.
Andrew	Look, you're awake now, so why don't you just let us have the food? Then we can give our guests a meal and you can go back to sleep. A loaf and a few eggs would be fine.
Joshua	You never give up, do you? Jess! Get them what they need and then we can go back to bed.
Jessica	*(Appears at base of pulpit with a carrier bag)* Here you are, Andy. What does that teacher friend of yours say? 'Ask and you will receive.' You knew that we wouldn't leave you stranded.
Andrew	He also says, 'Knock and it will be opened!' Thanks! Good night!

Andrew goes back to the house. Jesus addresses the whole congregation.

Jesus	So you see, my friends, your heavenly Father doesn't give you things because you are a good friend or deserve them. He gives you what you need because you ask for it. Those of you who are parents make all sorts of mistakes, but you know how to look after your children. Trust your heavenly Father to do even more and he will give you the very best when you ask him.

Finding out (20 minutes)

You may find that the children have lots of questions to ask about prayer. If so, leave out the drama and use the time for discussion. Try to be honest and say when you don't know the answer. Also admit that we all find praying difficult at times. The children may want to ask why God apparently does not answer prayers for people who are ill or starving. There are no 'right' answers to this, but the following points may be helpful.

- We may try to explain gently to people in distress— for example, a little girl whose father has died—that he was very ill and suffering, that this suffering has now stopped but God knows that she misses him.
- Problems of starvation are often down to war and bad economics; God does provide our basic needs, but people often use them badly. We are generally well off in this country and we can provide help.
- Sometimes God answers prayers in different ways than we expect but we do not realize it until a long time later.

Finish by saying that we have to help in God's work by being his hands and feet for him.

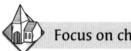

Focus on church

If there is a prayer board or book in the church, draw the children's attention to it. Remind the children that every service in church always includes praying for other people.

Worship

Music

Ask! Ask! Ask! And it shall be given (JP 11)
Cross over the road (CP 70)
Jesus' hands were kind hands (SSL 33; JP 134)

Prayer

Have to hand the two shoe boxes or ice cream containers. Give each child two slips of paper and a pencil. Ask them to think about anything that they want to thank God for, write it on a slip and then put it in the 'Thank you' box to be read out later. Then ask them to think of someone in need, write the person's name on a slip and put it in the 'Please' box. Tell the children that you will be reading out some of the prayers, but make it clear that nobody will know who has written which prayer.

Light the candle and sit around it. Open the 'Thank you' box and slowly read out some of the thanksgivings that the children have written. See that you treat each one as a special offering, even if it is unusual or appears frivolous. Ask the children if there is something else for which anyone wants to thank God.

Next, turn to the 'Please' box and do the same. At the end, allow a little time for the children to pray in silence and then sum up the prayers by leading the Lord's Prayer.

Speak to the children quietly to remind them to complete their task for next week or just to say 'Thank you' and 'Goodbye'.

Tasks

1. Ask the children to complete Unit 6 in the activity book.
2. Give each child an invitation card for the service 'Celebrating God's forgiveness', to take home.

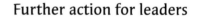

Further action for leaders

- ❖ Ask if the children can be involved in the prayers in church if they are not already.
- ❖ Follow up any questions about charities that may have come up. Does the church have one that it supports, or does it help with a local project?
- ❖ Liaise with your priest or minister about the service 'Celebrating God's forgiveness', which will be held soon after the next unit.

Unit 7

Sorry!

Aim

To teach that when we do things that are wrong, we can turn back to God to seek his forgiveness and restore our loving relationship with him.

Objectives

❖ To learn that we make dozens of choices every day and that some involve choosing between what is right and what is wrong.
❖ To recall that Jesus was like us, even to the point of being tempted to do and say things that are wrong. This is called 'sin'.
❖ To recognize that wrongdoing damages our relationship with God and with each other.
❖ To understand that God is waiting to forgive us, and that, through his grace, we can turn to him in sorrow and acknowledge the things we have done wrong before him.

I believe

I believe in Jesus Christ… who was crucified, died, and was buried… I believe in the forgiveness of sins.

SESSION 1

Biblical basis

Luke 4:1–13

Preparation and resources

You will need:
❖ A copy of the 'Choices' game board on page 91 for each child
❖ Counters (one per child)
❖ A copy of the questions for the 'Choices' game photocopied from page 92

As prayer is a vital part of the teaching in this unit, there is a section for worship in each session. See that you leave ample time for it.

Before you start

As the children arrive, take time to look at their activity books. Go through the last section, 'Thank you; please', carefully to see that the children have taken on board the idea of experiencing the presence of God and being able to praise and thank him as well as asking for things that concern them. This work will be recalled as we learn about praying for ourselves.

Teaching time (10 minutes)

Start by recalling some of the points about friendship that the children discussed during Units 4 and 5. Draw out that someone can be a good friend by helping you when you are in trouble, even though he or she may not be a person you play with. Remind the children of the story of the good Samaritan in Unit 4. Emphasize that the first two people chose not to help the person who had been robbed, but that the Samaritan chose to help, even though he did not know the man.

Game: Choices (15 minutes)

The 'Choices' game is similar to 'Snakes and Ladders', but is not intended to be competitive. Each player has a board and a counter. The leader reads out a question. The players decide which of the two or three options they would take. The leader then directs the players to move their counters forward or backward according to their choice of answer. Depending on the age and type of group, you could let the children give answers aloud or let them decide silently which to do.

When you have finished, ask the children which word kept coming up: 'choose'. Point out that we make choices all the time. Some of them concern things like what to eat or wear. We either choose them ourselves or our parents choose for us. (Refer to questions 1–3.) Some decisions are small, like choosing a cake to eat. Some are very big, like choosing where to live or go to school. Others are about the way we behave towards God and other people—whether we choose to do what is right or what is wrong. (Refer to questions 4–10.)

Read the story of Jesus' temptation, using the version below or a children's Bible. Remind the children that after Jesus was baptized, he went away into the desert for a long time to think about what God wanted him to do. This is what happened:

After spending a long time without food, Jesus was hungry. Then the devil came to him and said, 'If you are God's Son, order this stone to turn into bread.'

Jesus answered, 'Scripture says, "Human beings cannot live only on bread."'

Then the devil took Jesus to the top of a mountain and showed him the whole world and its greatness. 'I will give you all this if you will kneel down and worship me.'

Then Jesus answered, 'Scripture says, "Worship the Lord your God and serve only him!"'

Then the devil took Jesus to Jerusalem and put him on the highest tower of the temple. He said, 'If you are God's son, jump off, because scripture says, "God will order his angels to hold you up so that not even your feet will be hurt when you land on the ground."'

Jesus answered, 'Scripture also says, "Don't tempt the Lord your God."'

Then the devil left Jesus alone.

BASED ON LUKE 4:2–13

Finding out (15 minutes)

Briefly, relate the story to some of the questions in the game as follows:

- Jesus could have turned the stone into a loaf when he was hungry. Relate this to questions 5 and 8, which are about dishonesty.
- Jesus could have used the devil's power to rule the world. Relate this to questions 6 and 7 on bullying or fighting.
- Jesus was tempted to impress people by jumping off the temple. Relate this to questions 4 and 8 on trying to impress or cheating.
- Questions 9 and 10 are about loving God and loving your neighbour. Relate them to the summary of the Law: 'Love the Lord your God and love your neighbours as much as you love yourself.'

We are often tempted to do things that are wrong. We call wrongdoing 'sin'. We do this when we forget to love God, other people or ourselves. Jesus knows how hard it is to avoid sinning. We have just heard the story about a time he was tempted to do wrong.

Remember that just as we ask God to help other people who are in need, we can also pray for ourselves. When we say the Lord's Prayer, we say, 'Lead us not into temptation, but deliver us from evil.' Explain that God will help us to be strong to resist temptation, just as Jesus grew strong when the devil tempted him. It does not mean that we will always get it right, but with God's help, we can try!

Worship

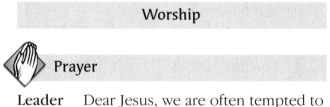

Prayer

Leader   Dear Jesus, we are often tempted to do the wrong thing instead of the right one. Help us to be strong and to choose the right thing to do. Amen

To finish, either say or sing the Lord's Prayer together.

Biblical basis

Mark 14:26–31, 66–72

Preparation and resources

Write the instructions for the role-play drama below on cards if the children are going to prepare it on their own.

Teaching time (10 minutes plus the drama)

Drama (10–15 minutes)

Start with at least one of the following pieces of simple role-play. Either ask the children to act it out first with directions and then act it again so that everyone is clear what is happening; or divide the children into two groups. Give each group a card with the instructions for one of the pieces of role-play, or ask adult leaders to work with the children. Each group rehearses the role-play and then acts it out to the other group.

He hit me first!

1. Two children are walking towards each other.
2. As they pass, one accidentally brushes against the other.
3. The other child deliberately gives a big shove in return, nearly knocking the first child over.
4. It turns into a fight (only acted!)
5. A third person appears and says, 'Stop fighting.'
6. The third person asks what happened. The children explain.
7. Both children say 'Sorry' to each other and walk off together.

A bit of a mess

1. A child is writing in an exercise book.
2. He or she looks out of the window, waves to friends, writes very fast, then runs out.
3. The child comes back with the teacher, who says, 'Show me your work.'
4. The teacher says, 'This is an awful mess. You can do much better work than this.'

5. The child says, 'I'm sorry.'
6. The teacher replies, 'That's all right. Now turn on to a new page and start again.'

Ask the children what happened in the pieces of role-play. Draw out that the children had behaved badly, then they realized or had it pointed out to them that they had done something wrong. They said they were sorry, became friends and started again.

Read the story of Peter's denial, using the following version or a children's Bible. Remind the children that there are times when we behave badly or let down even our family or best friends. This story is about Peter, who promised always to be friends with Jesus, even if everyone else left him. Jesus knew that he had many enemies and that the time was coming when he would be arrested by the people who wanted to stop him telling others about God.

Jesus and his friends were walking towards the Mount of Olives when Jesus said, 'All of you are going to run away and leave me.'

Peter answered, 'I will never leave you, even though all the rest do!'

Jesus said to Peter, 'I tell you, Peter, that before the cock crows twice tonight, you will say three times that you do not know me.'

Peter answered even more strongly, 'I will never say that, even if I have to die with you!'

Later that evening, Jesus was arrested by soldiers and taken to the high priest's house. Peter followed at a distance. He went into the courtyard and sat down with the guards, keeping himself warm by the fire. He was still in the courtyard when one of the high priest's servant women came past him. When she saw Peter warming himself, she looked straight at him and said, 'You are a friend of Jesus of Nazareth.'

But Peter denied it. 'I don't know... I don't understand what you are talking about,' he answered and went out into the passage. Just then, a cock crowed.

The servant woman saw him there and began to repeat to the people standing around, 'He is one of them!' But Peter denied it again.

A little while later, people accused Peter again: 'You must be one of them. You come from Galilee.'

Then Peter said, 'I swear that I am telling the truth! May God punish me if I am not! I do not know the man you are talking about!'

Just then a cock crowed a second time.

Then Peter remembered that Jesus had said to him, 'Before the cock crows twice, you will say three times that you do not know me.' And he broke down and cried.

BASED ON MARK 14:26–31, 66–72

Finding out (15 minutes)

In a brief discussion, draw out the following points:

- It is often difficult to admit that we have done something wrong, especially if we have also been hurt or angry.
- Sometimes, like Peter, we are so sorry for what we have done that we may cry or want to cry. Other times, it is hard to say 'Sorry'.
- Ask: When people who have been unkind to us say they are sorry, how do we feel? Is it easy to forgive them and become friends again?

When we say the Lord's Prayer, we say, 'Forgive us our trespasses as we forgive those who trespass against us' (or, if you use a modern version, 'forgive us our sins as we forgive those who sin against us'). Explain that we want people to forgive us when we do things that are wrong, but then we must be willing to forgive people who say 'sorry' to us.

Even when we are sorry that we have done wrong, we sometimes have to accept punishment. This may be something like missing a treat or it may be that a friend does not trust us for a while. That shows how serious sin is. It spoils things. It puts up a wall between God and us. But Jesus, by dying on the cross for us, broke down the wall. If we tell God we are sorry that we have not loved him or other people, he loves us so much that he forgives us and lets us start again. The Church has Jesus' authority to assure us of God's forgiveness (John 20:21–23). This is often called the Absolution or Prayer of Forgiveness.

If your church uses the sacrament of Reconciliation, this would be the time to teach about it.

Discussion starters

1. **You must own up. I will come with you.**
   Ben stole a chocolate bar from the sweet shop. His mum was very upset when she found out. She made Ben take the wrapper back, tell the shopkeeper he had stolen the chocolate, and pay for it. Ben's mum went with him because he was scared.

2. **Here are some flowers to say I am sorry I was rude.**
   Hannah was rude to an elderly lady. Hannah's dad made her pick some flowers from the garden and take them to her instead of watching television. After Hannah had apologized, she and the elderly lady became friends.

- Why was Ben's mum upset?
- What did Ben have to do to put things right?
- How did his mum help him?
- What did Hannah do to apologize to the elderly lady?
- What happened as a result?
- What was the cost to Hannah's dad?

Points to draw out

- Ben and Hannah had to show they were sorry as well as saying so.
- Ben's mum and Hannah's dad also suffered because their children had done something wrong. Ben's mum was very upset and she probably paid for the chocolate. Hannah's dad gave the flowers from his garden.
- They both helped their children to put things right because they loved them and wanted them to learn from their mistakes.

Explain that God, our heavenly Father, is like a good parent. He is sad when we do things that are wrong. He also suffered for all the wrong things that we do, by letting Jesus die on the cross for us. If we tell God we are sorry that we have not loved him or other people, he loves us so much that he forgives us and helps us to start again.

We will be celebrating this in a service on … (give date). We will all have a chance to tell God how sorry we are for the things we have done wrong and to celebrate his forgiveness and a new start.

Focus on church

In some church services we start by remembering all the things we have done wrong and telling God we are sorry. In others, this may not happen until later in the service. In some churches, people may say or sing a very old Christian prayer: 'Lord have mercy, Christ have mercy, Lord have mercy.' In others we may be reminded of the summary of the Law: 'Love the Lord your God and love your neighbours as much as you love yourself.' In all of them, we will then hear a prayer in which we are reminded that if we are sorry, God will forgive us. It does not matter which format you use in your church. What matters is for the children to recognize it and feel able to join in.

Worship

Music

Father, I place into your hands (CHE 159; JP 42)
Father, lead me day by day (JP 43)
The Lord's Prayer *(Caribbean)* (CP 51; CHE 584; JP192)

Prayer (5 minutes)

Sit quietly with the lit candle or the cross as a focal point. If you wish, play some quiet music. Ask the children to think about anything that they have done wrong today and to tell God about it in the silence of their hearts.

Leader Lord God, we have done things today that were wrong. Lord, we are sorry.

All Lord, we are sorry.

Leader For the times that we have been unkind to people by saying things or fighting…

All Lord, we are sorry.

Leader For the times that we have not helped people who have needed our help…

All Lord, we are sorry.

Leader For the times we have wasted the good things that you give to us…

All Lord, we are sorry.

Leader For the times that we have not forgiven people who have been unkind to us…

All Lord, we are sorry.

Leader Thank you, Lord, for forgiving us when we are sorry, and letting us be your friends again. Amen

Either say or sing the Lord's Prayer together.

Tasks

1. Encourage the children to spend a few minutes at the end of each day, thinking through the things that they have said and done. When they have said and done things that were wrong, they can tell God that they are sorry and ask for his help to do better. It is just as important to recall the opportunities for doing good things and the times when they have resisted temptation, and to thank God for them.
2. Complete Unit 7 in the activity books.
3. Remind the children that this unit is linked with the service when we will celebrate God's forgiveness. Give each of them a note with the date and time to take home to their parents.

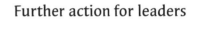

Further action for leaders

❖ Go through the preparation section in the chapter 'Celebrating God's forgiveness' to see that everything has been done.
❖ Ensure that there is publicity about the service on your notice sheet.
❖ Arrange a meeting for the leaders and clergy to look at the 'Initial preparation' section of the chapter on planning the first Holy Communion service.

Celebrating God's forgiveness

Aim

To help the children to reflect on the wrong choices they make and experience God's forgiveness while deepening their understanding of Christ's death and resurrection.

Objectives

❖ To use the story of Peter's denial to illustrate the pattern of sin, sorrow and forgiveness.
❖ To illustrate that sin comes between us and God, and that it is through the cross that the barriers are broken down and we can be restored to him.
❖ To value the freedom and new life that spring from knowing of God's forgiveness.

THE SERVICE

This act of worship, or one of your own design, should take place some time after the children have studied Unit 7. It forms part of their preparation for receiving Holy Communion. The idea of a congregation meeting together to reflect on their sins and celebrate God's forgiveness is new for many churches, but is increasingly used as part of the preparation for Easter and Christmas. This may be an opportunity to introduce it in your church, but take care to see that the service is designed for the children with the adults joining in, rather than the other way round. Whatever plans you make, hold the service at a time when the parents and sponsors can be present to support the children.

If the children are going to receive Holy Communion at Easter, it is worth leaving this service until some time in Holy Week so that it can be linked with Jesus' crucifixion and resurrection. Unlike the 'Welcome and presentation of Bibles' and the first Holy Communion service, which are celebrations for the whole community within the Sunday worship, this service stands alone and is by its very nature more low-key and intimate. Remember to give it just as much care with decoration of the church and use of music as a normal Sunday service. If only the children and their parents are to be present, or if it is a very small group, the act of worship should be kept very relaxed with an informal commentary. As it celebrates God's forgiveness and anticipates the 'big day', have some refreshments afterwards, while the 'sins' are burned, to end on a note of festivity.

Preparation and resources

The aim is to show how our sins come between us and God, but that Jesus' sacrifice on the cross breaks down the barriers and allows us to become God's children by adoption.

You were dead, because you were sinful and were not God's people. But God let Christ make you alive, when he forgave all our sins. God wiped out the charges that were against us for disobeying the Law of Moses. He took them away and nailed them to the cross.
COLOSSIANS 2:13–14

Now that we are his children, God has sent the Spirit of his Son into our hearts. And his Spirit tells us that

God is our Father. You are no longer slaves. You are God's children, and you will be given what he has promised.

GALATIANS 4:6–7

Place either the altar table or a similar table in a central point with a large cross or crucifix on top of it. At the foot of the cross or crucifix, either place pieces of paper on which people have written the things they have done wrong, or create a 'wall of sin' around it. In either event, the 'sins' will be burnt after the service is over.

You will need:

❖ Either a large basket, such as a laundry basket, to collect the pieces of paper, or a 'wall' made from a large sheet of brown paper with brick outlines drawn on it

❖ Adhesive tape

❖ Pencil and piece of paper for each person

❖ A large rubbish sack

❖ Newspaper-style headlines of the sins of the world, showing crimes such as war, murder and fraud

❖ Pots of flowers

Either:

1. Place the basket with the open rubbish sack inside it in front of the altar table.

Or:

2. Make the wall of sin by using brown paper with a few rough outlines to give the impression of bricks or stones. Fasten the wall around the altar table so that it comes above the top of it, to partly obscure the cross.

3. Stick the newspaper-style headlines of the sins of the world to the basket or the wall.

4. Give a pencil and paper to each member of the congregation as they arrive.

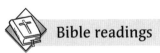

Bible readings

The service is based on the story of Peter's denial of Jesus, his sorrow and then Jesus' forgiveness and commission (Mark 14:27–31, 53–54, 66–72; 16:1–7; John 21:15–17, 19b). The readings form an integral part of the action so they should be read informally with no introduction to break the flow of the service.

If you choose to write your own act of worship, there are other stories that could be used, such as Zacchaeus, the prodigal son, or the lost sheep.

Prayers

Most of the prayers are responsorial so that everyone can join in easily. They are deliberately short and informal so that they can be used with young children, but they may not suit an older group. Write your own if you wish to fit your church's particular tradition and needs.

Music

Use quiet taped or organ music during the building of the 'wall of sin', or the silence may become oppressive and cause people to hurry unnecessarily. Many Lent and Easter hymns and songs would be appropriate as well as the suggestions that are made in the service outline below.

ORDER OF SERVICE

Opening hymn or song

Amazing grace (CHE 40; JP 8)
Peace, perfect peace (CHE 597; CP 53)
Praise, my soul, the king of heaven (CHE 602; JP 204)
Seek ye first the kingdom of God (CHE 633; JP 215)
When Jesus walked in Galilee (CP 25)

Introduction

The priest or minister introduces the service in the following or similar words:

Dear friends, we are all happy that you are nearing the time when you will meet Jesus in receiving Holy Communion. Before you take that step, it is important that you remember how Jesus died on the cross to free us from our sins—the things we do wrong—so that we can live as his sons and daughters.

Either:

To show how our sins come between us and God, we have a basket placed between us and the cross. During the service, we shall all be invited to write our sins and the sins of the world down on the paper provided and put it in the basket. By dying for us on the cross, Jesus broke down the barriers. To symbolize this, we shall take the basket outside after the service and burn the pieces of paper that are in it.

Or:
To show how our sins make a barrier between us and God, we have started to build a wall between us and the cross. During the service, we shall all be invited to write our sins or the sins of the world down on the paper provided and add it as a brick to the wall. By dying for us on the cross, Jesus broke down the wall. To symbolize this, we shall tear up the wall and put it in a rubbish sack. After the service, we shall take it outside and burn it.

Now, we are going to think about Jesus' friend, Peter. Peter promised to follow Jesus, but he denied even knowing him a few hours

later. After the resurrection, Jesus forgave Peter and he became the great apostle who travelled all over the known world to teach people the good news.

 ### First Bible reading

Jesus said to his disciples, 'All of you will reject me, as the Scriptures say, "I will strike down the shepherd, and the sheep will be scattered." But after I am raised to life, I will go ahead of you to Galilee.'

Peter spoke up, 'Even if all the others reject you, I never will!'

Jesus replied, 'This very night before a cock crows twice, you will say three times that you don't know me.'

But Peter was so sure of himself that he said, 'Even if I have to die with you, I will never say that I don't know you!'

MARK 14:27–31a

Prayer

Priest/minister Jesus, we want to be your friends but, like Peter, we make promises that we do not keep. We let you down by not loving God or other people. Help us to remember the things that we have done wrong that have hurt you and our friends, and to be sorry for them. Amen

Follow this prayer by using the petitions from Unit 7, or make up your own.

Second Bible reading

This reading is a retelling of the events from Mark 14.

Jesus was taken to the high priest's house. Peter followed from a distance and went into the courtyard of the high priest's house. One of the high priest's servant women came by. She looked straight at him and said, 'You, too, were with Jesus of Nazareth.'

But he denied it. 'I don't know him. I don't

understand what you are talking about,' he answered and went out into the passage. Just then a cock crowed.

The servant woman saw him there and began to repeat to the bystanders, 'He is one of them!' But Peter denied it again.

A little while later. the bystanders accused Peter again, 'You can't deny that you are one of them, because you too are from Galilee.'

Then Peter said, 'I swear that I am telling the truth! May God punish me if I am not! I do not know the man you are talking about!'

Just then a cock crowed a second time.

Then Peter remembered how Jesus had said to him, 'This very night before the cock crows twice, you will say three times that you don't know me.' And he broke down and cried.

BASED ON MARK 14:26–31, 66–72

The worshippers are invited to move to quiet places around the church and are given time to write their sins or the sins of the world on the pieces of paper. When each person is finished, he or she either sticks the paper on the wall or puts it into the basket. During this, quiet music is played. Be helpful by either briefing a few adults to take a lead or by encouraging anyone who is hesitant with a smile or a gesture of invitation.

Prayer

Priest/minister (or together) Dear Jesus, like Peter, we have let you down by not loving you or other people. Like Peter, we are sorry. Forgive us and make us your friends again. Amen

The priest or minister says the following prayer for forgiveness, or a similar one.

Priest/minister God of mercy and power, heal our sins, forgive our faults and give us your grace to walk with you today and every day, through Jesus Christ our Lord. Amen

The priest or minister either moves the basket away to the side of the church or tears down the wall and puts it in the rubbish sack. The children may place flowers near the cross to symbolize the new life that we receive through God's forgiveness.

Songs or hymns to sing during the above activity

Cleanse me from my sin, Lord (JP 27)
God forgave my sin in Jesus' name (CHE 209; JP 54)
I was lost but Jesus found me (JP 125)
Joy is the flag flown high (JP 144)

Third Bible reading

After the Sabbath, Mary Magdalene, Salome, and Mary the mother of James bought spices to put on Jesus' body... The women went into the tomb, and on the right side they saw a young man in a white robe sitting there. They were alarmed.

The man said, 'Don't be alarmed! You are looking for Jesus from Nazareth, who was nailed to a cross. God has raised him to life, and he isn't here... Now go and tell his disciples, and especially Peter, that he will go ahead of you to Galilee. You will see him there, just as he told you.'

MARK 16:1, 5–7

Pause, or use another reader.

When Jesus and his disciples had finished eating, Jesus asked, 'Simon son of John, do you love me more than the others do?'

Simon Peter answered, 'Yes, Lord, you know I do!'

'Then feed my lambs,' Jesus said.

Jesus asked a second time, 'Simon son of John, do you love me?'

Peter answered, 'Yes, Lord, you know I love you!'

'Then take care of my sheep,' Jesus told him.

Jesus asked a third time, 'Simon son of John, do you love me?'

Peter was hurt because Jesus had asked him three times if he loved him. So he told Jesus, 'Lord, you know everything. You know I love you.'

Jesus replied, 'Feed my sheep...' Then he said to Peter, 'Follow me!'

JOHN 21:15–17, 19b

Reproduced with permission from *Welcome to the Lord's Table* published by BRF 2006 (1 84101 504 0) www.barnabasinchurches.org.uk

Prayer

Priest/minister 'Now go and tell his disciples, and especially Peter, that he will go ahead of you to Galilee. You will see him there, just as he told you.' Let us pray: Risen Christ, thank you for letting us meet you here today.

All Thank you, Lord.

Priest/minister As you forgave Peter, so too do you forgive us. Thank you for letting us experience your forgiveness. Lord, you know we love you.

All Thank you, Lord.

Priest/minister Thank you for calling us to follow you. Help us to choose to do right, rather than wrong.

All Thank you, Lord.

Priest/minister Now, just as for Peter, you have work for us to do. Let us go out to love and serve the Lord.

All In the name of Christ. Amen

Final hymn or song

Follow me, says Jesus (JP 46)
I will be with you (CHE 289)
When Jesus walked in Galilee (CP 25)

Reproduced with permission from *Welcome to the Lord's Table* published by BRF 2006 (1 84101 504 0) www.barnabasinchurches.org.uk

Jesus is risen

Aim

To discover the meaning of Jesus' resurrection.

Objectives

❖ To hear and discuss the story of Jesus' resurrection.
❖ To explore a few of the questions about the resurrection story.
❖ To understand the importance of celebrating Easter.

I believe

I believe in Jesus Christ… On the third day he rose again; he ascended into heaven, he is seated at the right hand of the Father.

SESSION 1

Biblical basis

Mark 16:1–7; John 20:1–10

Preparation and resources

You will need:
❖ The Ready Box for the craft activity
❖ A poster made of blue and green paper to represent a bare landscape, or a bare branch and some thread. (Use the one saved from the Jesse tree in Unit 2)
❖ Outlines of spring flowers, young animals and eggs
❖ Two pictures showing winter and spring scenes or bare and leafy trees (see pages 93 and 94)
❖ A dormant bulb and a flowering one, or seeds and plants

Display the pictures of winter and spring and the bulb and flowers.

Before you start

As the children arrive, ask them to prepare for the session by thinking and telling each other about a time when they had a big surprise.

Teaching time (20 minutes)

Start by asking the children if they have ever had a surprise—a time when something lovely happened that they did not expect. Answers will probably include opening a present and finding that it was something really special, or arriving home to find an unexpected visitor.

Keep hold of any that are a mixture of sadness and joy. For example, there may be stories about someone who has been ill in hospital suddenly getting better and coming home unexpectedly; or doing a test and feeling really upset because it was hard, but then finding that they had passed.

Ask the children how they felt when these things happened. Draw out that often we may say nothing at first: we just look and take it in. Then we are excited and want to tell people all about it. Point out that although some of their surprises happened a long time ago, they were important enough to be remembered still.

Show the children the pictures of winter and spring (pages 93 and 94). Ask them what are the signs of spring after a cold winter: warmer weather, leaves on trees, flowers growing, baby animals, sunshine, longer days? Some of these are signs of new life. Show the children the bulb or seeds and then the new plants. The bulb or seeds look dead and dull but they grow into beautiful flowers and leaves.

Remind the children that Jesus died on the cross for us, and that made us all very sad. But just as we have had situations when sad things ended happily, so did this. Relate it back to any of the surprises that the children told, which had this pattern. We believe that death was not the end of Jesus. He came to life again and promised to be with us always.

Tell the story of Jesus' resurrection by using the following version from Mark's Gospel, or reading the story from a children's Bible. Alternatively, you may wish to use the more familiar version from John 20:1–10. If you use a children's Bible, read the story in two parts to correspond with the two teaching sessions.

NB: The resurrection narratives vary across the four Gospels. Mark's version was chosen for the service celebrating God's forgiveness because, in Mark's account, the angel singled out Peter in his message. Therefore, the same version is given here. You may prefer to use the more widely known version from John's Gospel, which is continued in the reading for the second session in the unit.

If the children have taken part in 'Celebrating God's forgiveness', remind them that they heard the resurrection story during the service. If they have not had the service yet, briefly remind them of the story of Jesus' crucifixion and his burial in a tomb, which would have been like a small cave.

After the Sabbath, Mary Magdalene, Salome, and Mary the mother of James bought some spices to put on Jesus' body. Very early on Sunday morning, just as the sun was coming up, they went to the tomb. On their way, they were asking one another, 'Who will roll the stone away from the entrance for us?' But when they looked, they saw that the stone had already been rolled away. And it was a huge stone!

The women went into the tomb, and on the right side they saw a young man in a white robe sitting there. They were alarmed.

The man said, 'Don't be alarmed! You are looking for Jesus from Nazareth, who was nailed to a cross. God has raised him to life, and he isn't here. You can see the place where they put his body. Now go and tell his disciples, and especially Peter, that he will go ahead of you to Galilee. You will see him there, just as he told you.'

MARK 16:1–7

Finding out (5 minutes)

Mark's Gospel

1. How do you think these women felt when they found that the tomb was empty?
2. Do you think the women believed the young man?
3. What do you think they did next?
4. What do you think Peter thought when the women gave him the angel's message?

John's Gospel

1. How do you think Mary Magdalene felt when she found that the tomb was empty?
2. What do you think Peter and the other disciple (John) thought when she told them that Jesus' body had been taken from the tomb?
3. What do you think Peter thought when he saw the empty tomb but the burial wrappings lying there?

Do one of the following activities.

Craft: new life display (15 minutes)

NB: As this is a corporate activity, it is easier to have the basic poster pinned up so that the group can see what they are creating.

1. Display the background poster, which is a bare landscape—the top third blue, and the rest green or brown.
2. Invite the children to choose from the cut-outs of examples of new life: spring flowers, leaves on trees, eggs hatching into chicks and so on.
3. Colour the pictures and stick them on to the poster. You could add a picture of the empty tomb like the one in the activity book.

4. Make a heading: 'New life at Easter' or 'Thank you, God, for new life'.
5. As an alternative, make a 'new life' tree by decorating a bare branch with the cut-outs attached with loops of thread.

Game for older children: Which version is right? (15 minutes)

If you read a different version of the resurrection story from the one used in the service, some of the children may have picked up the fact that the two stories are not the same. Some may have remembered other versions anyway. Explain that when stories are passed on, especially when people are very excited, they can get altered.

1. Put the children in pairs. Ask one to tell his or her partner six things about their family and themselves.
2. Then get the partner to tell the group the six things they heard.
3. Did he or she get it absolutely right?
4. Now swap round and do it again.

If the children know each other very well, try doing the same game with a subject like 'Six things about my last holiday', or 'Something special that happened to me'. Show that nobody got their report completely wrong but that they made little alterations. The stories of Jesus' resurrection were passed on by the apostles telling other people, and were not written down until about 40 years after the resurrection happened, so it is natural that each one will be different. What matters is the part that they all have in common: the tomb was empty and the disciples were so convinced that Jesus was alive again that they went all over the world telling people about it.

SESSION 2

Biblical basis

John 20:11–18

Preparation and resources

1. If you have a garden or churchyard, and it is the right time of year, see if there are either caterpillars or butterflies to show to the children. Alternatively, find some pictures of caterpillars and butterflies.

2. Collect a few pictures of yourself throughout your life, as a baby, toddler, teenager, and adult. If you don't have any, borrow a book from the library containing pictures of a famous person.

Teaching time (20 minutes)

If possible, start by taking the children outdoors to look for either caterpillars or butterflies. Depending on which you find, ask either how the butterfly started life or what the caterpillar will eventually become. You will probably find that the children know all about this in great detail. If you have a younger group and can't find any caterpillars or butterflies, you could read *The Very Hungry Caterpillar* by Eric Carle (Puffin) as a light-hearted alternative. If that is not appropriate, show pictures of caterpillars and butterflies.

Emphasize that the butterfly looks totally different from the caterpillar—it flies and has brightly coloured wings, whereas the caterpillar is furry and crawls slowly—but it is still the same creature. It looks outwardly different but is still inwardly the same.

Show the children the pictures of yourself throughout your life. Be prepared for giggles about your appearance as a baby or the different fashions in clothes. Although you have changed a great deal—you can walk, have grown hair or, maybe, lost it again, are fatter or thinner—you are still the same person inside. You have the same talents and feelings about some things that you have had all of your life. Some of the children may observe that they saw a relative after a few years and did not recognize him or her at first.

Read a little more of the resurrection story. Recall that three women had gone to Jesus' tomb and been amazed to find that his body was not there. An angel had told them that he was risen. The story continues:

Mary Magdalene stood crying outside the tomb... Then she turned around and saw Jesus standing there. But she did not know who he was. Jesus asked her, 'Why are you crying? Who are you looking for?'

She thought he was the gardener and said, 'Sir, if you have taken his body away, please tell me, so I can go and get him.'

Then Jesus said to her, 'Mary!'

She turned and said to him, 'Teacher.'

Jesus told her, 'Don't hold on to me! I have not yet gone to the Father. But tell my disciples that I am going to the one who is my Father and my God, as well as your Father and your God.' Mary Magdalene then went and told the disciples that she had seen the Lord.

JOHN 20:11a, 14–18

Finding out (15 minutes)

- Mary did not recognize Jesus. Can you think why?
- What did Jesus say that made her recognize him?
- What did he tell her not to do?

There are all sorts of reasons why Mary may not have recognized Jesus: it was still dark; she was crying; she did not expect to see someone who was dead. Draw out that although Jesus was alive and still the same person, his resurrection body was different; a little bit like the way a caterpillar becomes a butterfly.

Point out that Jesus told Mary not to hold on to him. She wanted to keep him there with her for ever, but this was not possible. He was going to return to heaven to be there in glory with his Father, God. (Can anyone remember a story when Peter wanted to make a special moment with Jesus last for ever?)

Mary recognized Jesus when he called her by name. He knows all of our names, and he calls us by them, too.

Focus on church (15 minutes)

Ask the children why we have most of our church services on Sunday. You may get all sorts of answers, but pull out the real one—that it is the resurrection day. We meet as God's family to worship a risen Christ. Every Sunday is a sort of mini-Easter.

At Easter we do all sorts of things to celebrate that Jesus is alive. We use symbols of new life: flowers, water, candles, maybe a special Easter or Paschal candle, because the living flame reminds us that Jesus is alive. We give Easter eggs as a symbol of new life. Many of the hymns we sing contain a special word: 'Alleluia!' This means 'Praise God!' What do you do at your church to show that Easter is special?

Worship

Prayer

Sit quietly with the lit candle or the cross as a focal point. Play some quiet music. Praise Jesus for being risen and with his Father but also close to us when we pray. Ask the children if there is anything anyone wants to thank God for. If there is a time of hesitation, add your own thanks, or leave them to the end. Then ask the children if there is anything they want to tell God about or ask him. If there is a time of hesitation, add your own petition, or leave it to the end. Finish by saying the Easter greeting, 'Christ is risen, Alleluia!' or singing an Easter song. Make it sound really joyful!

Music

Any traditional hymns about Easter would be suitable. The children will probably also know the following songs.

Alleluia! Give thanks to the risen Lord (CHE 32; JP 3)
God is love (CHE 215; CP 36)
God's not dead (no), he is alive (JP 60)
I danced in the morning *(Lord of the dance)* (CHE 275; CP 22; SSL 29; JP 91)
We have a king who rides a donkey (SSL 51; JP 264)
When Jesus walked in Galilee (CP 25)

Tasks

1. Ask the children to complete Unit 8 in their activity books.
2. Check that everyone has brought back the reply giving the number of people who will be coming to the first Holy Communion service.
3. Give out a reminder of the date of the rehearsal, which also asks parents to see that the activity books are tidied up, with any unfinished work completed and tatty covers mended.

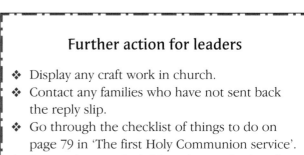

Further action for leaders

- ❖ Display any craft work in church.
- ❖ Contact any families who have not sent back the reply slip.
- ❖ Go through the checklist of things to do on page 79 in 'The first Holy Communion service'.
- ❖ Discuss how each child can be involved in the first Holy Communion service and where it is appropriate for parents or sponsors to help.

Let's have a party

Aim

To teach the significance of the sacrament of Holy Communion.

Objectives

❖ To experience the symbolism of the Passover meal (the old covenant).
❖ To learn about the story and promises of the last supper (the new covenant).
❖ To link the old and new covenants with the death and resurrection of Jesus.

I believe

I believe in Jesus Christ… who was crucified, died, and was buried…
   On the third day he rose again.

SESSION 1

Biblical basis

Exodus 12; 13:2; Mark 14:12–16, 22–26

Preparation and resources

You will need for the Passover activity:
❖ Paper or plastic plates and glasses
❖ Lamb bone (a cardboard one will do)
❖ Parsley
❖ Salt water
❖ Matzos or water biscuits, folded in a napkin
❖ Radishes
❖ Honey
❖ Blackcurrant or other red fruit juice in a glass jug
❖ Candles

Have a table laid with a white cloth, candles, and a plate and glass for each child. The parsley, salt water and radishes should be in dishes, with the matzos folded in a napkin. It is easiest to serve the 'wine' from a glass jug.

Before you start

The children will probably be excited or curious when they see a table laid for a meal. Explain that they are going to celebrate a special party during this session. Let them look at the items and ask questions about them.

Teaching time (20 minutes)

Start by asking the children about the event they learned about in the last unit.

• What do we call the time when we celebrate Jesus' resurrection?
• What do we do at Easter to show that it is special?
• What do we do when something special happens? We have a party! Easter is the biggest Christian party.

Talk for a few minutes about some of the parties the children have enjoyed: birthdays, weddings, fireworks, New Year and so on. What special food did they eat?

What did people drink? Point out that all parties include special food and drink. What do people eat at particular kinds of parties: fireworks parties, weddings, Christmas and so on?

Some people have parties every year on the anniversaries of birthdays or weddings, or on New Year's Eve. Perhaps your whole family meet for Christmas dinner or your friends come for a party or a treat on your birthday. Explain that the Jewish people have a special meal called the *Seder* every spring, when the whole family meets together to celebrate the Passover, the time when God delivered them from slavery in Egypt into freedom in the promised land. This was God's covenant with his people and he commanded them to keep the feast every year for ever. Read the story of the Passover meal.

If you have a group of older children and a leader who is a talented storyteller, consider reading the whole story, which is found in Exodus chapters 11—14.

God said, 'Choose a lamb that is big enough for each household. Roast it and eat it with bitter herbs and bread made without yeast. Eat it quickly, for you are to be dressed for travel with your sandals on your feet and a stick in your hand. It is the Passover festival to honour the Lord. You must celebrate this as a festival to remind you of what I the Lord have done.'

And the Lord brought the Israelite tribes out of Egypt. Moses said to them, 'Remember this day... Celebrate this festival every year for ever.'

ADAPTED FROM EXODUS 12:5–14, 51; 13:5, 10

Drama: A simple ceremony using some of the Passover rites (20 minutes)

Follow the reading by doing as much of the drama activity as is possible. Acting out some of the elements of the *Seder* will underpin much of the meaning of the last supper.

The Passover meal (*Seder*) is normally celebrated at home with the whole family present. The celebration revolves around the telling of the story (*Haggadah*). By hearing the story retold, each generation is brought into God's plan. Each Jewish person has been liberated by God, just as his or her ancestors were. Before the Passover, the whole house is cleaned, and leaven (anything made from yeast) is removed. The table is laid with special dishes, candles and food. A place is left empty for the prophet Elijah.

Sit the children around the table. Explain that the Passover meal is very long, but we are going to eat and drink some of the special food, as it was part of the Jewish meal that Jesus shared. It can be re-enacted in three ways:

1. Give each child a part to read on a numbered card so that, with prompting from you, they can read and act the parts themselves.
2. Use adults to read the mother's and father's part and share the part for the youngest child out between the children.
3. Read it all yourself and give directions for the various actions. This is not so dramatically effective, but is better if the children do not read fluently or if time is limited.

1. Introduction

Mother	*(Lights the candles)* Blessed are you, Lord, God of all creation. You have made us holy through your commandments. You have commanded us to light these festive candles. Bless our homes: Let your face shine upon us in blessing and peace in our hearts.
Father	Today the Jewish people celebrate Passover: they recall their liberation from slavery in Egypt; they recall Moses their leader; they recall above all how God intervened to save them.
Mother	The first act of Passover is Kiddush, a blessing. *(All the glasses are filled)* Let us stand for the blessing cup: Blessed are you, Lord, God of all creation: through your goodness we have this wine to drink.
All	Blessed be God for ever.

Everyone drinks.

Mother	*(Lifts a sprig of parsley)* This is a sign that nature comes to life in the spring. I shall dip it into salt water, a reminder of the bitter tears in Egypt.

Blessed are you, Lord, God of all creation: through your goodness we have all the fruits of the earth.

All   Blessed be God for ever.

Everyone eats the parsley.

Mother   *(Taking up the matzos)* This is the bread of affliction which our fathers ate in the land of Egypt. Let all who are hungry come and eat!

Mother breaks off a piece of the matzos, eats it and passes the rest around the table. All eat matzos.

2. The first question

Youngest child Why is this night so different from all other nights?

Father   This night is special because the Jewish people celebrate that God rescued Israel through Moses.

If time allows, read Exodus 12:1–8, 11–14.

3. The second question

Youngest child Why do we eat bitter herbs on this special night?

Father   We eat bitter herbs because our fathers were slaves in Egypt and their lives were made bitter. Let us now take some bitter herbs and eat them.

Radish is passed around and eaten.

4. The third question

Youngest child Why do we eat bitter herbs again, but this time dipped in haroseth?

Father   We dip bitter herbs into haroseth, a sweet paste, as a sign of hope.

Everyone dips the radish into honey and eats it.

5. The fourth question

Youngest child Why do we eat lamb when we celebrate Passover?

Father   This reminds us of the lamb which our fathers were instructed to sacrifice at the Passover meal when they were freed from Egypt. Blood from the lamb was marked on the doorposts. This was a sign for the angel of death to pass over their houses. So the lamb is eaten as a memorial of the saving acts of God.

6. The fifth question

Youngest child Why do we eat unleavened bread and drink wine at Passover?

Father   Our fathers ate unleavened bread because they had to leave Egypt in a great hurry. There was not time to wait for the yeast to rise so they baked unleavened bread, matzos, the bread of affliction, the bread of poverty, made only of flour and water.

Many cups of wine are shared at Passover. Wine is drunk in honour of the Law, the giving of God's word in the commandments. We drink it to honour the covenant between God and his people. Another cup is drunk in honour of Elijah the prophet and there is a seat reserved for him at table for when he returns to herald the Messiah.

After the drama is completed, remind the children that we learned in Unit 2 that Jesus and his family always went to Jerusalem for Passover time, and so he would have had a meal like this every year (Luke 2:41–50). When he was a small boy, he would have learned how it celebrated the rescue of God's own people from the slavery of sin and death, to live in freedom in the promised land. That was the covenant, the promise that God made with his special people. In the next session, we shall learn how Jesus used the Passover meal with his friends to give us the new covenant.

Reproduced with permission from *Welcome to the Lord's Table* published by BRF 2006 (1 84101 504 0) www.barnabasinchurches.org.uk

SESSION 2

Biblical basis

Mark 14:16, 22–25

Preparation and resources

You will need:

❖ The Ready Box
❖ Plain postcards or similar sized pieces of card
❖ Communion vessels

Before you start

Go through the activity books with the children as they arrive. Point out any pages that need tidying or completion. Have the communion vessels on display so that the children can see and handle them.

Teaching time (20 minutes)

Start by reminding the children of the fifth question at the Passover meal: 'Why do we eat unleavened bread and drink wine at Passover?' Explain that we are going to find out how Jesus used the bread and wine of the Passover at the last meal he had with his friends before he died.

Read the story of the Last Supper, using the version below. Alternatively, tell the story from a children's Bible.

It was the first day of the Festival of Thin Bread... Jesus' disciples asked him, 'Where do you want us to prepare the Passover meal?'

Jesus said to two of the disciples, 'Go into the city, where you will meet a man carrying a jar of water. Follow him, and when he goes into a house, say to the owner, "Our teacher wants to know if you have a room where he can eat the Passover meal with his disciples." The owner will take you upstairs and show you a large room furnished and ready for you to use. Prepare the meal there.'

The two disciples went to the city and found everything just as Jesus had told them. So they prepared the Passover meal...

During the meal Jesus took some bread in his hands. He blessed the bread and broke it. Then he gave it to his disciples and said, 'Take this. It is my body.'

Jesus picked up a cup of wine and gave thanks to God. He gave it to his disciples and said, 'Drink it!' So they all drank some. Then he said, 'This is my blood, which is poured out for many people, and with it God makes his agreement. From now on, I will not drink any wine, until I drink new wine in God's kingdom.'

MARK 14:12–16, 22–25

Finding out (10 minutes)

The old covenant saved the Jewish people from slavery in Egypt. Jesus gave us the new covenant. He saved us from the slavery of sin and death by dying on the cross for us, and gave us the freedom of new life with him. We do not just remember this as the last meal before he died, but that he is risen. We can share in his risen life through meeting him in Holy Communion.

Jesus told us to do this in memory of him. He also commanded us to love each other: 'I tell you to love each other, as I have loved you' (John 15:12). When we obey Jesus' commands, we are close to him, and we are also close to each other as we share the meal that he gave us in the Eucharist. He invited his disciples to share in this special party. He also invites us to this party—or his banquet—given in his honour every Sunday when we celebrate the Eucharist.

- If the Queen invited you to a banquet, how would you feel?
- What would you do to get ready?

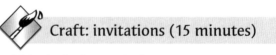

Craft: invitations (15 minutes)

Make invitation cards that say:

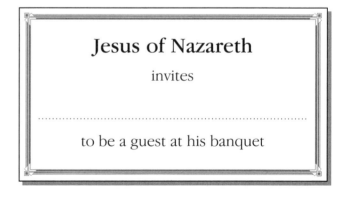

> # Jesus of Nazareth
>
> invites
>
> ....
>
> to be a guest at his banquet

Ask each child to fill in his or her name and decorate the card.

Reproduced with permission from *Welcome to the Lord's Table* published by BRF 2006 (1 84101 504 0) www.barnabasinchurches.org.uk

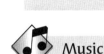

Focus on church (15 minutes)

Look at the vessels used in Holy Communion. Take them into church and place them on the altar table. We have an altar table in an important place in the church because it is used for the meal that Jesus gave us. In some churches, it is very much like an ordinary large dining table. In others, it has a white cloth and a brightly coloured frontal in different colours according to the season of the year. At Easter it will be white or gold.

The early Christians were baptized and received Holy Communion for the first time at Easter. The children may be following their example by doing the same, but every Sunday is a celebration of Easter when Jesus rose from the dead. Ask the children again, 'What do we do at Easter to show it is special?' We have a party! Easter is the biggest Christian party!

Worship

Music

Any Communion hymn would be suitable. You may also consider:

From the darkness came light (CP 29)
Take our bread we ask you (*We are yours*) (CHE 678)
When Israel was in Egypt's land (*Let my people go*) (CHE 803; JP 276)

Prayer

Light the candle or sit quietly looking at the cross. Say a Christian version of the Passover Prayer:

Leader Blessed are you, Lord, God of all creation: through your goodness we have this bread to offer, which earth has given and human hands have made. It will become the bread of life.

All Blessed be God for ever.

Leader Blessed are you, Lord, God of all creation: through your goodness we have this wine to offer, fruit of the vine and work of human hands. It will become our spiritual drink.

All Blessed be God for ever.

Then continue:

Leader Blessed are you, Lord, God of all creation: through your goodness we have ourselves to offer, created by you, loved by you. Take us and make us your own.

All Blessed be God for ever.

Finish by singing a song or hymn.

Tasks

1. Ask the children to complete the task for Unit 9 in their activity books and to see that it is tidied up before the next session.
2. Allocate any readings or tasks for the first Holy Communion service so that the children have plenty of time to learn them or to find out how they will be involved in the service.

Further action for leaders

Ask each of the children to bring a small photograph of themselves for the display they are making next week, or bring a digital camera to take them yourself.

NB: Parents should be asked for permission before putting their children's photographs on display. If a parent is not willing to give permission, let the child draw a picture instead.

Let's share a meal

Aim

To teach that we meet Jesus in Holy Communion.

I believe

I believe in the Holy Spirit… the holy catholic Church.

Objectives

❖ To link the last supper with the present-day Eucharist.
❖ To discuss some of the elements of the Eucharist.
❖ To understand that we, the Church, are also the Body of Christ.

SESSION 1

Biblical basis

1 Corinthians 11:23–25

Preparation and resources

As we are nearing the end of the course, there will be all sorts of things that you may want to include in this session. The children may have questions that they want to ask, or there may be subjects that need fuller discussion. Remember that there is another unit after they have received Holy Communion, so save some of the answers until then.

Some of the children may be used to attending the Eucharist and seeing their parents or older friends receiving Holy Communion. These children may be very familiar with the service. Others may have only attended a Eucharist occasionally. In this case, you may want to spend more of the teaching time going through the service. In order to make this flexible, the only practical activity is making a display for the church, which shows the children as part of the Body of Christ. This can be spread across the two sessions as time permits.

You will need:
❖ The Ready Box
❖ Attractively presented bread and grapes, or crisps and fizzy drinks

For the 'Vine and branches' display:
❖ Brown paper (or adapt the Jesse tree from Unit 2)
❖ Bright green paper to make vine leaves

For the 'Living stones' display:
❖ Large piece of wallpaper with an outline of a church building
❖ Self-adhesive labels measuring about 75mm x 50mm

NB: In order to save time, draw the outline of the vine or the church building before the session begins.

Before you start

If you are planning to do the 'Vine and branches' display, invite the children to cut out the vine leaves. If you are doing the 'Living stones' display, ask the children to think about the names of members of the congregation, mission links and other local congregations as well as saints who are linked with your church. Check that you have a photograph (or drawing) of each child.

Teaching time (10 minutes)

Start by recalling that we learned about two meals in the last unit, the Jewish Passover meal and the last supper that Jesus celebrated with his friends. Point out that eating food together is a sign of friendship. Ask the children:

- Who do you sit with for lunch at school?
- Who do you share sweets or crisps with?

If someone new comes to live next door, your parents may invite them in for a meal or a drink. Having a meal together cements friendships. Wine is very important in the Passover meal. It was such a special drink that the Jewish people were called 'God's vineyard'. Explain if necessary that wine is made from grapes, which grow on vines. In the Old Testament, the prophet Isaiah uses the imagery of a vineyard to describe God's relationship with his people: 'I am the Lord All-Powerful! Israel is the vineyard, and Judah is the garden I tended with care' (Isaiah 5:7a).

In the New Testament, Jesus uses the same image. He speaks of himself as a vine. He said to his friends, 'I am the vine, and you are the branches… You did not choose me. I chose you and sent you out to produce fruit, the kind of fruit that will last' (John 15:5, 16). (This text may have been used at the 'Welcome and presentation of Bibles'.)

Jesus called Peter a 'rock'. He said, 'So I will call you Peter, which means "a rock". On this rock I will build my church, and death itself will not have any power over it' (Matthew 16:18). Peter called his Christian friends 'living stones'. He wrote, 'And now you are living stones that are being used to build a spiritual house' (1 Peter 2:5).

So we are all joined to Jesus and each other like the branches of a vine or the stones of a building.

Craft

Start making one of the following displays to decorate the church.

The vine (20 minutes)

1. From sheets of brown paper, cut a vine-shaped tree with bare branches. Fix it to the wall or mount it on a large sheet of paper, which is then hung on the wall. Alternatively, adapt the Jesse tree that you made in Unit 2.
2. Make large vine leaves out of bright green paper.
3. Ask each child to write his or her name and put a photograph or a drawn 'photograph' on a leaf.
4. Staple the leaves to the tree.
5. Write the heading, 'I am the vine, and you are the branches' (John 15:5).

Living stones (20 minutes)

1. Draw an outline of a church building on a piece of wallpaper. Make it look as much like the basic shape of yours as possible. Sketch in a few brick outlines.
2. Using self-adhesive labels as bricks, add names of members of the congregation, local churches, and mission links, as well as the names of saints to remind us that we are all part of the same Church on earth and in heaven.
3. Ask each child to write his or her name and put a photograph or a drawn 'photograph' on a large brick made of two or three labels.

4. Stick the bricks on to the building.
5. Write the heading, 'And now you are living stones that are being used to build a spiritual house' (1 Peter 2:5).

Finish the craft about ten minutes before the session is due to end. Sit down quietly, and remind the children how we learned at the beginning of the session that having a meal together cements friendships. Read the following Bible passage. Introduce the reading by explaining that Paul was a great leader and teacher who taught many people about Jesus. He often sent letters to groups of Christians to teach them more about Jesus and to tell them how to behave. This is what he wrote to the Christians in Corinth:

I have already told you what the Lord Jesus did on the night he was betrayed. And it came from the Lord himself.

He took some bread in his hands. Then after he had given thanks, he broke it and said, 'This is my body, which is given for you. Eat this and remember me.' After the meal, Jesus took a cup of wine in his hands and said, 'This is my blood, and with it God makes his new agreement with you. Drink this and remember me.'

1 CORINTHIANS 11:23–25

Finish the session by sharing the bread and grapes as a reminder of the bread and wine of Holy Communion. Alternatively, share crisps and fizzy drinks.

SESSION 2

Biblical basis

Luke 24:13–34

Preparation and resources

You will need:
- ❖ The Ready Box
- ❖ The 'Vine and branches' or 'Living stones' display that you started in the first session
- ❖ Vessels and other items that are used at Holy Communion
- ❖ Bread and wine

1. Do any necessary work on the display so that you can complete it during this session.

2. Arrange the Communion vessels, bread and wine, and any robes or vestments on a table.

Before you start

Encourage the children to handle the items used at Holy Communion and to ask questions about them before the session starts.

Teaching time (10 minutes)

Remind the children that Jesus has promised always to be with us. When he broke the bread at the last supper, he told his friends to do this in memory of him. We will recognize and come close to Jesus when we receive Holy Communion.

Read the story of Jesus' appearance on the road to Emmaus. The Gospel reading is quite long, so either use the version below or tell the story from a children's Bible. Older children might enjoy the version used in chapter 1 (page 7). Think back to Jesus' resurrection. He had appeared to the women but everyone else thought that he was dead. This is a story about two of his friends who were walking home on the Sunday evening, the same day that Mary and the other women had been sure that Jesus was alive.

On Sunday evening, two of Jesus' friends were walking to a village called Emmaus, which was near to Jerusalem. As they went along, they were talking sadly about what had happened. Then Jesus joined them. Somehow, they did not recognize him.

Jesus asked them, 'What are you talking about?' They were surprised that he did not know what had happened, but they explained that Jesus, their leader, had been imprisoned and then killed. They had been sure that he was the promised king who would rescue them from the Romans. They had felt that this was the end of all their hopes, but that morning some women had gone to his tomb and had found it empty. They had come back saying that an angel had told them that he was alive, but nobody had seen him.

Then Jesus said that they had not

understood what it was all about. He explained how the scriptures had said that all this would happen.

By this time, it was evening and they had arrived at their home. Jesus was going on, but they said, 'Stay with us; it is getting dark,' so he went in to stay with them. As they sat down for the meal, he took the bread and blessed it; then he broke it and gave it to them. They suddenly recognized him. It was Jesus! Then he disappeared.

The two friends said to each other, 'Didn't we get excited when he explained the scriptures to us?' They rushed straight back to the disciples in Jerusalem and told them, 'Jesus is alive. We recognized him when he broke the bread with us!'

BASED ON LUKE 24:13–34

Finding out (15 minutes)

1. Why were the two friends sad?
2. When Jesus joined them, they did not recognize him. Can you think why?
3. What did Jesus do that made them recognize him?

Recall that Mary Magdalene, too, had not recognized Jesus when she first saw him. The disciples had also assumed that Jesus was dead, so they did not expect to see him and, somehow, his resurrection body made him look different. The two friends recognized Jesus when they shared a meal with him. He took bread, blessed it, broke it and gave it to them. Then they realized that he would be with them whenever they did this to remember him.

We cannot see Jesus now because he is with his Father in heaven, but he has promised always to be with us by sending his Holy Spirit to guide and strengthen us. We recognize him in the same way as his friends did, when he speaks to us through the Bible and when we share in the bread and wine at Holy Communion. When we go to the Eucharist, there is a lot going on that we can think about. Ask the children for ideas. Draw out that:

- We meet as God's family to share in the meal Jesus gave us, just as Jesus and his friends enjoyed having meals together.
- We remember that Jesus died on the cross to free us from sin and death.
- We thank God for the good things he gives us and pray for the needs of the world.

- We recall the past; the last supper that Jesus shared with his disciples.
- We think about today; that Jesus is risen and present with us in Holy Communion.
- We look to the future; that one day we will join with Jesus in a banquet in heaven.
- We are like branches on a vine, which will produce fruit if we obey Jesus' command to love each other.

After we have received Holy Communion, we may feel wonderful or we may feel just the same. We believe that Jesus is close to us and loves us, so spend some time being still and talking to him in your own words.

Craft

Finish the 'Vine and branches' or 'Living stones' display.

Finding out: What's in a name? (10 minutes)

The children may ask why Christians give different names to the service when we receive Holy Communion. Use a few minutes to explain that they all reflect parts of the service:

- We gather as God's family.
- We thank him.
- We remember what Jesus did.
- We go out to serve him

It does not matter which name we use. They all come from parts of the service that Jesus gave us.

1. Some people call the service Holy Communion. Communion means 'togetherness', so the name reflects people gathering as God's family.
2. The name most commonly used is Eucharist, which means 'thanksgiving'. The prayer when we recall what Jesus did for us is the prayer of thanksgiving, the eucharistic prayer.
3. Some Christians call the service the Lord's Supper, when we remember what Jesus did and commanded us to do.
4. A very old name is the Mass. This comes from the Latin for the dismissal at the end of the service: 'Go out to love and serve the Lord.'

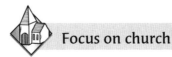

Focus on church

Use the last part of the session to talk about the items used in the service. Let the children practise taking and eating the bread and wine in the way that they will receive it in church, so that they are familiar with the taste and feel when they have the rehearsal. Answer any questions about the Communion vessels and other items and practices. If your church uses vestments, explain that they are copies of what a Roman gentleman would have worn in Jesus' time. Talk about the symbolism of the various colours that are used. See that the children are present for Holy Communion on the next Sunday if they are not there each week.

Worship

 ### Music

Give me yourself, O Jesus Christ my brother (CHE 192)
I will bring to you the best gift I can offer (CP 59)
Lord, we ask now to receive your blessing (JP 301)
One more step along the world I go (CP 47; JP 188)

 ### Prayer

Leader   Blessed are you, Lord God of all creation, for bringing us to this moment when we will receive Holy Communion. We pray for each other.

At this point, the leader could name each person by turn or each child could name the person next to him or her.

Leader   Hear our prayers in the name of Jesus our Lord. Amen

Tasks

1. Ask the children to complete the tasks in their activity books and to bring them to the first Holy Communion rehearsal.
2. Spend a little time answering any queries about the service. It is important to keep it as relaxed as possible, but it is only natural that the children will be nervous as well as excited about the event.

The first Holy Communion service

The service in which the children receive Holy Communion for the first time involves the whole Christian community. For the children, it is one of the most important moments in their lives, and their excitement and joy will be shared by their families. For the congregation that has supported them through the time of preparation with teaching, encouragement and prayers, it is a time of celebration as young Christians join them around the Lord's table. It is worth investing time and thought into seeing that the service goes smoothly and is as relaxed as possible.

The organization for the service has been planned as if there is a group of about ten children. If the group is smaller, the preparation and involvement become much simpler.

Initial preparation

1. A few weeks before the service, ask the children how many special guests they will be bringing so that seating can be arranged. If a child has had help from a sponsor from within the congregation, see that he or she is included with the family.

2. See that each child is involved in the service in some way. If any parents are to be involved, use this as an opportunity to include those who do not come to church regularly.

3. Some children may already be singers or servers, and it is fitting that they should perform that ministry during the service.

4. Identify children with strong voices for the Bible readings.

5. Involve the other children with the intercessions or the presentation of the gifts.

6. Check that the person in charge of the flowers is aware of the special day. A family could provide or arrange some flowers as their contribution to the service.

7. Ask your social committee, if you have one, if it intends to provide some sort of party afterwards. If you plan to offer just the usual coffee and tea, make sure the people in charge are warned of the extra numbers.

Rehearsal

Arrange a rehearsal with the parents and children one evening during the week before the service. If you use a speaker system or plan to rearrange the chairs, see that these are in place.

You will also need Communion bread and wine, and copies of:

* *Common Worship Initiation Services (Amendments): Rites on the Way* (obtainable from Church House Publishing)
* The service books used by your church
* The readings
* Intercessions on cards
* Seating plan

It should not be necessary to provide service books for the rehearsal, as everyone should be familiar with it, but have a few copies available in case anyone is unclear about a point.

Go through the service in full, mentioning the items like hymns and sermon when they happen so that everyone is clear about the order and the parts when they will be involved.

Seating

According to the numbers and space, arrange for the children to sit in the front rows with their parents and sponsors, or as a group, with their parents and sponsors seated immediately behind them. Be sensitive to family situations and make sure there is space reserved for other members of the family so that nobody is isolated. Use the rehearsal to get the families into the right order so that people can move easily to take part in readings, prayers and the presentation of gifts. If any children are singing or serving, see that they rehearse from those places.

Readers and intercessors

Give the readers an opportunity to practise coming forward to the lectern or pulpit, reading aloud and moving back to their seats. Make the readings available so the readers can practise them beforehand.

Children leading the prayers can each be given their prayer on a card or be asked to write their own on a particular subject. If they are writing their own, tell the parents so that they can provide any help that is needed. It is most straightforward if the children stand in a group around the lectern and move a step forward to the microphone to read. Give the children a chance to rehearse this in full.

Presentation of gifts

At this point, the children may be presenting their activity books as a symbol of offering themselves. This could be done as part of a procession with the bread, wine and money, or it could be done more simply by the children coming out of their places and placing their books in front of the altar table. Whatever you decide to do, see that it is fully rehearsed.

Rite of admission

It is not obligatory to have a formal rite of admission. The introduction to the service, readings, prayers, preaching and involvement of the children make it clear what is happening. On the other hand, many congregations would want some form of words to mark the occasion and to inform the new communicants of their support and friendship.

The Church of England has produced its own rite of admission, which has been commended for use by the House of Bishops. Copies of this rite, entitled *Common Worship Initiation Services (Amendments)* can be obtained from Church House Publishing. Visit www.chpublishing.co.uk for more information.

If you decide to write your own ceremony, it is appropriate to recall the children's baptism in some way and remind them that they have reached another stage in their Christian journey. This can be done in several ways:

- Renewal of baptismal vows.
- Processing from the font to stand before the altar table.
- Lighting of baptismal candles.
- Having the 'Path of Life' frieze that you made made in the first session prominently displayed, with a large arrow saying, 'You are here' or 'Today' pointing to the stage marked Holy Communion.

NB: Avoid using baptismal water or laying on of hands during the rite, as this could confuse the ceremony with baptism or confirmation.

It is important for the rite to be seen to be a solemn occasion as well as a celebration, but guard against demanding promises from the children that no adult communicant would be required to make. It is only through the generosity and grace of God that any of us is able to approach his table.

The children could be welcomed during the greeting at the beginning of the service or before the Peace. Whatever you decide to do, see that the text is written out and that it is fully rehearsed. Any responses should be loud and clear.

Communion

Explain and rehearse how the children and their families will be receiving Holy Communion. It is important for parents to come forward with their children, even if they are not receiving Communion. If it is the practice to offer a blessing to non-communicants, use this opportunity to inform the parents of the procedure so that they feel at ease and can explain it to any of their family and friends. The easiest way for non-communicants to show that they do not wish to receive the bread and wine is to carry a service sheet to the altar rail. The children should practise holding out their hands to receive the consecrated bread. It is important that they should also practise handling the chalice and tasting some wine to familiarize themselves with it.

In churches where Holy Communion is administered to the people in their pews, the procedure is more straightforward.

Finish the rehearsal by asking if there are any questions, repeating any reminders, and giving a few words of encouragement.

Before the service

The service should be like a normal Sunday service but with space reserved for the children and their guests. There are only a few things to be done on the day:

1. See that there are people to welcome the families as they arrive and show them to their seats. Ask families to be in their places about ten minutes before the service starts.

2. Have someone on hand to indicate when people move for the readings and prayers, so that the service flows smoothly.

3. Have the certificates and any other gifts ready well before the service.

4. Check that the children have remembered to bring their prayers. If they have not, help the child to compose a prayer now. Should there be any signs of nerves, just remind the child calmly what he or she has to do, or go through the movements with them again.

5. It is natural that families will want to take photographs. Let them know when there will be opportunities so that the service is not disrupted by flashes and whirrs.

After the service

At the end of the service, the children could be invited to come forward to be congratulated by the congregation and receive their certificates. Then they could join the clergy in processing out of church.

Looking to the future: all that I am

Aim

To show that receiving Holy Communion is not the end, but the beginning of another stage on the Christian journey as Jesus' disciples.

Objectives

❖ To help the children to recognize the many gifts and talents that they can use in God's service.
❖ To explore the idea of taking the love of Jesus out into the world.
❖ To touch upon the work of the Holy Spirit within us.

I believe

I believe in the Holy Spirit, the holy catholic Church… and life everlasting.

Biblical basis

**1 Corinthians 12:12–21, 27–28;
Matthew 25:34–40**

Preparation and resources

1. Have ready the 'Path of Life' frieze.

2. Make a mental list of a few of each child's gifts and skills.

3. You will need the Ready Box.

4. Make and copy small 'Thank you' cards for the children to fill in.

5. If you are going to do the jigsaw activity, make a cardboard cut-out of a body. (Drawing round a small child or a doll is the easiest way to do this.) Cut it into pieces to make a jigsaw for the game. **NB**: Make two heads.

Before you start

As the children arrive, ask them to fill in and sign a simple card to their parents and sponsors to thank them for their support and prayers.

> Dear ....
>
> Thank you for your support and prayers during the time I was preparing to receive Holy Communion.
>
> Love from................................

Give the activity books back to the children. Say something individual about the service to each one of them, especially about any way in which they used their gifts or reached out to other people.

Teaching time (15 minutes)

Start by talking a little about the service. Encourage the children to say what they enjoyed and how they felt. If anyone was disappointed about something, be sympathetic, but point out gently that nothing in life is perfect and it was still a special day.

Lead on to asking why we are meeting after everyone has received Holy Communion. Draw out that it is a milestone on our Christian journey, not the end of it. We are now entering a new stage. Refer to the 'Path of Life' frieze that you made in the first session. After the 'First Holy Communion' date, there is an arrow pointing to 'Looking to the future'. That is where we are today.

Ask the children to think back to the first two sessions; look at these units in the activity books. We started with ourselves: every one of us is different. In the second unit we wrote down some of the things we could do. God has given each of us gifts. Some of them are things that we are good at doing, like playing football or singing; others are about the way we behave—being good at sharing things or keeping cheerful when life is difficult, and so on.

Ask the children to say what gifts and skills they think they have. We are often bad at saying the good things about ourselves and there is also a tendency to put academic gifts above practical ones. Be sensitive with the children who hesitate and be ready to tell them the gifts that you have noticed in them. Include attitudes to other people, like befriending the lonely and helping someone who is hurt or old. Now refer to the display you made in the previous unit:

- What did Jesus call his disciples when he said he was the vine?
- The branches of a vine are rather like the limbs of a body.
- Jesus is no longer on earth because he is with his Father in heaven.
- We are not just his friends, but also his body here on earth.
- We are Jesus' hands and his feet. His Holy Spirit lives in us to help us to do his work.

Read the following retelling of the letter that Paul wrote to the Christians in Corinth. Remind the children that they heard part of a letter that Paul wrote to the Christians in Corinth during the previous session. It was about the last supper. This is another part of the letter. Paul wrote it to explain about Christians being like limbs on a body.

Christ is like a body that is made up of many parts. If a foot said, 'I am not a hand so I am not part of the body', that would not be true. If the ear said, 'I am not an eye so I am not part of the body', that would not be true. If you only had eyes, how could you hear? If you only had ears, how could you smell? God made each part of the body just as he wanted it to be.

So, then, the eye cannot say to the hand, 'I don't need you!' The head cannot say to the feet, 'I don't need you!' All of you are Christ's body and each one is a part of it. God has given each one of us a special job to do.

BASED ON 1 CORINTHIANS 12:12–21, 27–28

Do one of the following activities.

Craft: Funny bodies (15 minutes)

Give each child one of Paul's statements and ask him or her to try to draw a body that is like it:

- With the feet detached from it
- Only an eye
- Only an ear
- Eyes instead of hands
- A head instead of feet

After the activity is completed, emphasize that all of the body is important. So are all our gifts. Some are noticed more than others, but God needs them all to do his work. If we say that some don't matter, it is like pretending that we don't need feet and would rather have two heads!

Game: Jigsaw (15 minutes)

- Give each child a piece of the jigsaw. If it is a very small group, give each child two pieces.
- Ask them to write their names and their gifts and skills on one piece.
- If they have more than one piece, ask them to write someone else's name and their gifts on a second piece.
- Have some done yourself, with the names of people known to the children and the gifts they use to serve the church: playing the organ, gardening, welcoming people and other jobs.
- Then put the pieces together to make a body.

Try demonstrating Paul's letter by taking off the feet and putting a second head there. Show that by pretending the feet do not matter, not only can the body not walk, but the person and gifts written on that piece of puzzle are lost. God has given each of us a job to do for him, however small it may seem.

Finding out: for older children (20 minutes)

God has given us these gifts. How can we use them to serve him in the world?

Read Jesus' words from the following version, or from a children's Bible. Explain that Jesus was talking about the time when his friends would meet him in heaven. He would be the king, sitting on a throne surrounded with angels.

Jesus said, 'When we all meet in heaven I will say to you, "Come in, my friends, and enjoy the kingdom as your reward. I was hungry and you gave me food, thirsty and you gave me a drink, I was a stranger and you welcomed me into your home. I had no clothes and you gave me something to wear. I was ill and you looked after me; I was in prison and you came to see me." Then you will answer, "Lord, when did we give you food because you were hungry? When did we give you a drink because you were thirsty? When did we see you a stranger and welcome you into our homes, or needing clothes from us? We don't remember your being ill or in prison and our visiting you. What do you mean?"

'Then,' Jesus continued, 'I will reply, "I tell you that when you did these things for anyone, however unimportant that person was, you were doing it for me."'

BASED ON MATTHEW 25:34–40

Ask the children to think about Jesus' words. When we do things for other people, we are also doing them for him.

Does the story remind them of anything that they have learned in the course? You may wish to mention:

- People who help us (Unit 1)
- Loving God and our neighbour (Units 5 and 7)
- Praying for other people (Unit 6)
- The story of the good Samaritan (Unit 4)

How can we do the things that Jesus said? Emphasize that children cannot ask strangers to stay, or visit people in prison, but that they can do similar things within their own lives. Let them make their own suggestions, but these may be of some help.

- 'I was hungry and you gave me food, thirsty and you gave me a drink; I had no clothes and you gave me

something to wear': Not wasting food. Saving the world's resources, such as water, oil and electricity. Supporting aid agencies and charities. Being prepared to share what we have.
- 'I was a stranger and you welcomed me into your home': Being friendly to people who are lonely or a child who has come from another school.
- 'I was ill and you looked after me': Helping at home when your mum is tired. Sending a card to someone who is unwell. Learning some first aid at Cub Scouts or Brownies.
- 'I was in prison and you came to see me': Visiting anyone who does not get out much. Telling a friend who does not know your town or village about things they can do. Listening to people who are unhappy. Asking if you can give a lift to a friend whose family does not have a car.

 ## Focus on church

In church we offer our money to do God's work. At the Eucharist we also offer bread and wine, which represents everything in our lives. Last Sunday (or whenever it was) we used our various gifts during the service. We may have offered our activity books. These were our ways of offering ourselves to God. This is not something we do once, but every day, and especially when we meet with other Christians to worship God.

Resourcing the next part of the journey

Lastly, see that the children have the equipment for the next stage of their Christian journey. Give them information about an ongoing group in Junior Church, membership of an after-school club or young communicants' group.

Worship

 ## Prayer

Light the candle and play some music.

Leader   Thank you, God, for all the gifts that you have given to us.

All   Thank you for my gift of…

At this point, each child in turn could thank God for a gift they have.

Reproduced with permission from *Welcome to the Lord's Table* published by BRF 2006 (1 84101 504 0) www.barnabasinchurches.org.uk

Finish by singing together, either 'Lord, we ask now to receive your blessing' (Junior Praise 301) or 'All that I am' (Celebration Hymnal 23), or by saying the following post-Communion prayer from *Common Worship*:

Almighty God,
We thank you for feeding us with the body and blood
of your Son Jesus Christ.
Through him we offer you our souls and bodies to be
a living sacrifice.
Send us out in the power of your Spirit to live and
work to your praise and glory. Amen

Music

All that I am (CHE 23)
Come, Lord Jesus, come (CHE 128)
Cross over the road (CP 70)
If you see someone lying in the road (JP 95)
Look out for loneliness (SSL 36)
Lord, we ask now to receive your blessing (JP 301)
O Jesus, we are well and strong (SSL 40)

The best gift I can offer (CP 59)
Think, think on these things (SSL 38)
When I needed a neighbour, were you there (CP 65; JP 275; SSL 35)

Further action for leaders

❖ Display the 'Body of Christ' work in the church.
❖ Think whether there are ways in which any of the children can use their gifts within the worshipping community.
❖ If it is not already common practice, consider ways in which the children can be involved in offering their work and activities to God during services.
❖ Arrange a date for an evaluation meeting for everyone who has been involved with the course.

Appendices

Love the Lord
your God.
Love your neighbours
as much as you
love yourself.

Luke 10:27

Your word is a lamp that gives light wherever I walk.

Psalm 119:105

If you keep on obeying what I have said, you are truly my disciples.

John 8:31

Choices

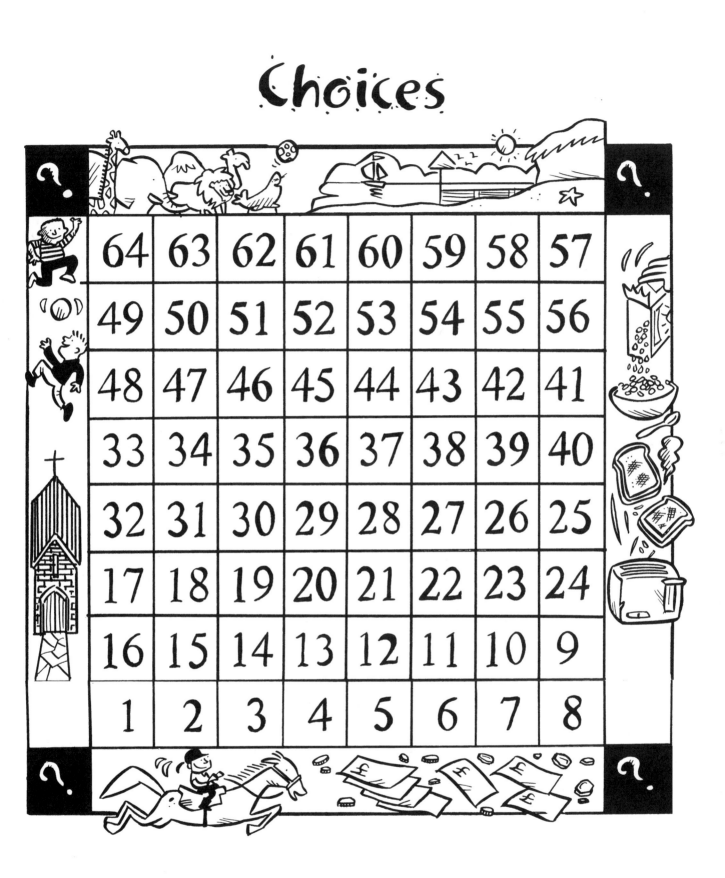

64	63	62	61	60	59	58	57
49	50	51	52	53	54	55	56
48	47	46	45	44	43	42	41
33	34	35	36	37	38	39	40
32	31	30	29	28	27	26	25
17	18	19	20	21	22	23	24
16	15	14	13	12	11	10	9
1	2	3	4	5	6	7	8

Terenure Branch Tel. 4907035

Choices

What would you choose?

1. You are going out for the day. Do you choose to go to the zoo or the sea?

Zoo..Go forward 6

Sea ....Go forward 6

2. For breakfast, will you choose to have cereal or toast?

Cereal..Go forward 6

Toast ....Go forward 6

3. When you go home, will you choose to read a book, play computer games or watch television?

Read a book ....Go forward 6

Play computer games.......................Go forward 6

Watch television..............................Go forward 6

4. Somebody at school says she has a pony and £1,000 in her bank book. Do you choose to say nothing or that you have a horse and £5,000?

Say nothing.....................................Go forward 6

Say you have a horse and £5,000 ....Go back 6

5. It is after school. You have no money and you are hungry. Do you choose to go home quickly for some food or take some sweets from the shop without paying?

Go home quickly..............................Go forward 6

Take sweets without paying..................Go back 6

6. There is a big fight in the playground. Do you choose to try to stop it, join in or tell a teacher so that he or she can stop it?

Try to stop it...................................Go forward 1

Join in ....Go back 5

Tell a teacher ....Go forward 8

7. Someone in your class has the kind of watch you've always wanted. Do you choose to bully them until they give it to you, hope to get one for Christmas, or say you don't like it?

Bully them ....Go back 6

Hope to get one ....Go forward 6

Say you don't like it ....Go back 5

8. There is a spelling test at school. You find spelling difficult. Do you choose to copy a friend's work, alter your answers, or do your best?

Copy a friend's work ....Go back 3

Alter your answers...........................Go back 3

Do your best ....Go forward 8

9. On Sunday a friend invites you to play. Do you choose to miss church or play afterwards?

Miss church ....Go back 6

Play afterwards ....Go forward 6

10. A little girl falls over in the playground. Do you choose to see if she is all right or run away?

See if she is all right ....Go forward 6

Run away...Go back 6

Reproduced with permission from *Welcome to the Lord's Table* published by BRF 2006 (1 84101 504 0) www.barnabasinchurches.org.uk

Welcome to the Lord's Table

Activity Book

Every page in this book has been designed to help you mark a very important journey. Step by step, it will help you to learn all about belonging to God's family. So it's about you and God.

You can fill in the pages by yourself, or with the help of a grown-up.

If you are using this activity book as part of your church's *Welcome to the Lord's Table* course, you will have the opportunity to offer it at your first Holy Communion as a sign that you belong to God and are part of his family.

ISBN 1 84101 044 8